PURPLE LEGION

Also by Christopher Keating

Purple Legion

Christopher Keating

For information, please visit http://www.chriskeatingauthor.com/

Original cover art by Samantha Byrum – http://mysweetvi66.deviantart.com/

First mass market edition

Printed in the United States of America

ISBN-13: 978-1539820307

ISBN-10: 1539820300

For Moonrabbit

For seven years, I dwelt
In the loose palace of exile,
Playing strange games with the girls of the island.
Now, I have come again
To the land of the fair, and the strong, and the wise.
Brothers and sisters of the pale forest,
Children of night,
Who among you will run with the hunt?
Now night arrives with her purple legion.
Retire now to your tents and to your dreams.
Tomorrow, we enter the town of my birth.
I want to be ready.

Jim Morrison
The Palace of Exile

Chapter One

"Who would have ever thought performing oral sex on a woman could kill you?"

Age had not caused Roger Tucci to lose his Mediterranean good looks. If anything, maturity had made him even more handsome. He still had his dark skin and, even in his mid-60s, only flecks of grey in his naturally dark hair and moustache. Men half his age wished they had his muscular physique. Women of all ages just wanted him and he had always been glad to accommodate them.

"Human papillomavirus. HPV," he read from the wall chart in the doctor's office. *It smells like a doctor's office*, he thought. If he been brought in blind-folded, the smell would have made him think he was in a doctor's office.

Dr. Takahashi gave Roger a few seconds to collect himself before continuing.

"An HPV infection that doesn't go away can cause cancer in the back of the throat, including the soft palate, base of the tongue and tonsils. The technical name is oropharyngeal cancer. 'Throat cancer' is a general term that covers a couple of other kinds of cancer, but it's good enough."

Roger had turned and was now looking out the office window, thinking about how lovely the blue sky was. "Is there any way to figure out when I got it?" He had been very calm as the doctor broke the news to him and he wasn't going to get excited now.

"By 'when' I'm assuming you mean *whom* did you get it from. That depends on how many partners you've had. This kind of cancer develops very slowly and may not be diagnosed until years, or even decades, after a person initially gets infected with HPV. Seven years would be a fair estimate of how long you've had it, but it can be much less or much more. If you've had more than one partner over your lifetime it probably wouldn't be possible to narrow it down. Even if you were to test every woman you've been with, they may have been infected then but are free now."

"What's the prognosis?" He could tell by the doctor's demeanor what the answer was, but he asked anyway.

"HPV-caused cancer is different than other forms of throat cancer and the prognosis is typically very good. If we had caught it early this kind of cancer would have been easily treatable. Your cancer is advanced, though. The real problem is it has spread

1

through metastasis and isn't just in the throat anymore. It's in your lungs as well. We could start a regimen of surgery and chemotherapy, but I'll be honest – your chances are not good. That kind of treatment is likely to reduce your quality of life while increasing your lifespan only a short while. I've put together some literature for you to review."

Tucci took the literature Takahashi was holding out and glanced at it.

"The fact you haven't already booked me for surgery tells me everything I need to know. How much time are we talking about?"

"That's hard to say. Six months, maybe less. You should get your affairs in order."

Tucci nodded his understanding. The doctor was being more honest than he probably should be. He interpreted the doctor's time estimate to be on the 'maybe less' side of things.

Roger was resigned to the situation. He had done his own research and had been pretty sure of the situation before he had first seen the doctor the week before. The problems had started with a sore throat some months earlier. Throat lozenges had helped and he hadn't thought anything of it. Then he developed some ear pain and a chronic cough, but Dallas can be brutal for allergies and he had had problems with his allergies before. Again, he treated it with over-the-counter medication and hadn't thought anything more about it. When his friends commented on the change in his voice and how he had been losing weight, Roger began to wonder. The throat lozenges weren't helping as much and he had developed problems swallowing. To top it off, he always felt tired. He did some searches online for his symptoms and what he found made him call Dr. Takahashi at the University of Texas Southwestern Medical Center for an immediate appointment.

Takahashi had examined his throat before taking a tissue sample for a biopsy and ordering a CAT scan. He had been very noncommittal at the time but Roger had become successful by reading people, and the doctor's body language was clear. He had known his fate long before the test results had come back – the results sitting now on Takahashi's desk.

"What can you do for me?" he asked.

"I can prescribe some treatment that will help some. I can also give you some pain killers. The pain will get worse, but that will be later. Right now, it will be manageable. I can also prescribe medication to relieve the ear problems and help you swallow. We can up the dosage as the cancer progresses. Eventually, you'll need to check into a hospital."

Roger waited while the doctor filled out the script. When Takahashi handed it over, Roger shook his hand and said, "Thank you, Doctor. I appreciate your help."

As he started to leave, he turned to the doctor and said, "In case you're wondering, let me tell you, it was worth it. There's nothing like making a woman scream in passion. What a great time!" And he left with a smile and low laugh.

As he made his way back to his office, he began a list of people he needed to call. His three children, his mother, a couple of business associates. He thought momentarily of calling his ex-wife, Kristen, and decided it wasn't a good idea. They had been on very bad terms ever since she had decided she wouldn't put up with his philandering anymore and had kicked him out of the house. He was afraid she would enjoy the news.

"Hey, Christmas is coming up," he said to himself. "Maybe I'll give her a present and tell her she's the one who gave it to me. *On the fifth day of Christmas my ex-wife gave to m,e h pe-ee-ee vee!* She would love it." Rationalizing his actions, he followed up with, "Of course, if there had been more screaming in passion and less plain old screaming things might have been different. I'll let the kids break the news to her."

But, there was one person in particular he needed to call – Patricia Kennealy.

§§§§§

In 1919, 31-year old Conrad Hilton traveled to Cisco, Texas to purchase a bank, but the deal fell through when the bank turned out to be too expensive. As Hilton was wondering what to do next, he became aware of the housing shortage due to all of the migrant workers attracted by the oil boom. Consequently, he purchased the 40-room Mobley Hotel and founded a business empire.

A town of about 4,000 in the middle of North Texas, Cisco is more reminiscent of the way things used to be in Texas rather than the way things are now in a twenty-first century city. Depending how you measured it, the drive from Dallas was either 130 miles, 2 hours or 50 years.

The heavy end-of-school traffic on Conrad Hilton Blvd had put her in a bad mood, and Patricia Kennealy silently cursed. The knowledge she had done it to herself didn't help. She knew she needed to go to the grocery store but had failed to take care of her chores earlier while the kids were still in school. She could only deal with it and live with the fact she had no one else to blame. Fortunately, the weather that October afternoon was pleasant and she was able to drive with the windows down. Texas summers could be brutal at times and winters had periods of bone-chilling cold, but the rest of the year was near perfect. She thought of how this afternoon was a classic example with mild temperatures and clear, blue skies.

She turned her pick-up truck into the parking lot of Brookshires, the closest thing they had to a grocery store, and her phone rang just as she was parking. The screen said it was Roger Tucci calling.

"Roger, what a nice surprise," she said as she answered.

§§§§§

Patricia Morrison's childhood in Dallas had been simple and routine with nothing more than her flaming red hair to set her apart from anyone else. She attended Southern Methodist University after graduating high school, majoring in horticulture with the intention of working in greenhouses. Along the way, she met John Kennealy.

He saw her while walking down the sidewalk one day. A panhandler approached her and was rebuffed, but that wasn't enough and he continued to follow her. Maybe it was her slim build and short height that made him think she was vulnerable, but when he continued to harangue her, he was caught off guard when she suddenly turned on him and berated him. She didn't stop there. As the panhandler tried to get away, she chased him down the sidewalk, loudly hurling insults at him until he was able to escape. The crowd on the sidewalk cheered her. All John could think was how beautiful she was and decided he wanted to meet the red-headed fireball.

Taking the chance he was going to get his face ripped off, he approached and asked if he could walk with her. To his surprise she agreed. She liked his dark hair and rugged good looks. They passed his destination and he kept walking with her until she

4

told him this was where she was going. He asked for her number and, on a whim, she gave it to him. She told him later his personality made her feel calmer. He understood. He was the anti-red-headed fireball and they made a good pair.

They got married three years later, right before graduation.

John was a hydrologist and got a job working in the Dallas office of the Texas Water Development Board after graduation. They were able to rent an apartment in Dallas's artsy M Streets, a short distance from the TWDB office, and they moved in right after their graduation with the typical youthful illusion of starting an idyllic life.

John's job began right away, but Patricia was still setting up their home before beginning her job and spent the day cleaning the apartment. The M Street area had very liberal standards and the warm May weather made her decide the idea of cleaning topless sounded refreshing, even when cleaning the balcony of their second-floor apartment, hidden behind a vine-covered trellis. That's when she found out the door to the balcony locked automatically when it swung closed, leaving her stranded with no way to get in and no way to contact John.

After reviewing all of her options, she resolved herself to climbing down the trellis on the outside of the building. Once on the street, she had to decide what to do next. Not wanting to let their new landlord see her like this, she brushed her long red hair over her small exposed breasts in the hope no one would notice and set off like Lady Godiva to find a payphone at the nearby convenience store.

Things were going well until she reached Greenland Hills High School with some of the students sitting outside while on their lunch break. Once they noticed the topless woman walking down the street the word spread quickly and before she knew it she was entertaining a raucous audience of whistling and cat-calling teenagers.

Changing her plan, she fled down a side street with laughter and whistling chasing her from behind, and rang the doorbell of the first house she came to, using her hands to cover her bare breasts. A medium-height, dark-skinned, middle-aged man of uncommonly good looks answered the door. Taking one up and down look at Patricia, he said, "Well, young lady. I think we need to find you something to wear."

She waited in the living room while he went to the bedroom and returned with a purple dress shirt, identical to one he was wearing, discreetly looking away while she put it on.

"Thank you so much. I got locked out of my apartment and was heading to the corner to call my husband on a payphone, but the kids at the high school started getting carried away."

"Can you blame them? They were just having a little fun, that's all. Listen, I'm having a late lunch with some friends in the garden out back. Use my phone there to call your husband and then come join us."

"I don't want to sound ungrateful..."

He interrupted her before she could finish. "I might remind you, those students are still out there and would probably love for you to make an encore."

She hesitated and he took the opportunity to hold out his hand.

"I'm Roger, Roger Tucci."

She took his hand and shook it.

"Patricia Kennealy. Pleased to meet you."

Lunch turned into storytelling and she was still there with Roger and his friends when her husband arrived after work. She and John became regulars in Roger's circle after that and they ended up becoming close. Roger, they learned, was a successful self-employed businessman who would build up a business before selling it for a handsome profit, simply to turn around and do it again. He would have been very wealthy except for the way he would burn through money with a lavish lifestyle, helping people out, and supporting various causes. Over the years, he made several offers to help Patricia and John, but they always turned him down. They spent time with him because they liked him – not because they liked his money.

The fly in the ointment was Roger's wife, Kristen. She had been more than tolerant of his escapades with women but a woman could stand only so much and she viewed Patricia as another of Roger's conquests. No amount of good behavior on Patricia's part was ever able to convince Kristen that Patricia wasn't sleeping with her husband. The irony was she was probably the only one of Roger's female acquaintances who wasn't. Kristen stayed with Roger for the sake of the children and the luxurious lifestyle he provided her. She would make the required appearances at parties and public functions and made the effort to present the face of a businessman's happy wife. Kristen Tucci wasn't the most pleasant of people, but no one could fault her for the effort she put into her role. When she split up with Roger she called Patricia and told her, "He's all yours now. I'm done with him." Patricia never heard from her again.

By that time, John and Patricia had moved to Cisco where John worked in the local hydrologic office. Life had been good to them and they raised a son and a daughter together.

Then, Roger told her he was dying.

§§§§§

"He wants me to be his power-of-attorney agent. That's the proper term, I learned."

She had broken the news to John after dinner when they were alone. She didn't want to discuss the news in front of the children. They were in the kitchen, together cleaning up.

"Why you?" he asked as he handed her a clean plate to dry.

"He didn't say, but I'm probably the only person he trusts. I may be the only woman he has ever known who never went to bed with him and we're the only friends he has who aren't holding a hand out for money. It has to narrow the list down."

"I always suspected he wanted to go to bed with you."

"Well you can quit suspecting because he did want to go to bed with me. Ever since I showed up at his front door with my tits hanging out."

"I'm sure he thought he had won the Lotto. Did he ever make a pass?"

"No. He was always a perfect gentleman. He never did anything improper with me. I could tell, though. It was flattering. He's such a good-looking guy. It was nice to have a man look at me like that every now and then."

John was a little hurt. "You mean I don't?"

"Oh, you sure do. That's the difference between us and him and Kristen. We're happy together. They never were."

John let the water drain out of the sink before asking, "What are you going to tell him?"

"If you're okay with it, I want to do it. He has always been a good friend to us. It will mean I'll be tied up with things at times. You and the kids will have to pick up the slack."

He thought about it and sighed as he answered. "You're right. He's a good friend and now he needs someone to help out. I'll talk it over with Greg and Chelsea. We'll be fine. Go take care of Roger."

"I won't have to do anything for a while. As long as he can make decisions for himself he won't need me. I'm sure it won't be too bad. I'm guessing he has everything in order."

John gave her a skeptical look before answering. "Dear, this is Roger Tucci we're talking about."

She slumped down a little and admitted, "Yeah, you're right. It's going to be a mess."

Interlude

They were walking together in the garden, surrounded by walls that kept it private. It was a beautiful house and well maintained, but not ostentatious. It allowed her to live luxuriously, without the appearance of being overly wealthy or attracting attention. She was using clippers to trim the flowering plants as they went, with the young man hanging on her every word. He found her gravelly voice incredibly sexy and easy to listen to.

It was a warm, late spring afternoon and she was wearing a light sundress with nothing on underneath. When the sunlight was right, he could see her lithe body through the fabric and felt himself getting aroused by the sight. Pleased with the way he was pretending to not look at her, she brushed a strand of her sandy blonde hair out of her face and made sure to stand with the sunlight coming from behind her to give him the best view possible.

"Remember, every one of our actions affects all living things," she told Roger. "When you do something - when you do anything - it starts a series of events that goes far beyond anything you can perceive or plan for. There are consequences for all of our actions."

She was handing him cut flowers as they went.

"If we can't know what happens, we can't plan for it, so why bother worrying about it?" Roger asked. "Couldn't you say taking path A is just as good as path B? If we don't know the consequences, how can we take those consequences into account when making our decisions?"

"That's the simple answer, but it's wrong. A certain level of awareness must take place before we can truly communicate with what is all around us. Once we realize there are consequences, we can use that knowledge in our decision-making. But, an important thing to remember is we are not talking about only ourselves. This is true of all things. Maybe the animals don't have the ability to see the consequences of their actions, but we can. I mean, we can see the consequences of their actions. For example, by careful observation and by paying attention, ancient medicine people learned from the animals which plants were edible and which were poisonous."

9

Roger sucked at his finger where it had been pricked by a thorn on the roses he was carrying.

"I'm missing the point," he told her.

"The actions of everyone around you will have consequences. By paying attention you can learn which actions are productive and which are poisonous. This not only can serve to make you better, but it will give you opportunities. By knowing actions will have consequences, you can be ready and you can profit in many ways."

"I think I see what you're trying to say."

"The world is a tapestry and it is being continually woven by our actions. If you observe the actions of those around you with a clear eye, you can see the weave and then, comprehending the tapestry becomes easy. The leaves dropping into the stream may think they are free to choose their path, but the current of the water will take them in an irresistible direction. It's the same thing with us. We are all in the stream of the community around us and the current of that community will work to sweep our decision-making in some particular direction. Put it all together and you can navigate the current instead of being swept by it."

She handed him a bunch of yellow flowers with a bright, red center.

"These are Coreopsis. They can really brighten up a room," she told him.

"The old saying knowledge is power is a true statement" she continued. "It all begins with the individual. You need to see people, which means more than just looking at them. Practice noticing details about people. Begin with some routine. When you meet someone, repeat their name to yourself and then say to yourself what color their hair is, what their clothes look like. Notice their posture and say it to yourself. 'This is Bob. His hair is brown. He's wearing a Beatles t-shirt. He's standing with his weight on one leg.' All of that means something. As you get better at it, you'll be able to add to the list of things you see and you'll learn to do it automatically.

"And, remember, everything is connected. By actually seeing someone, you'll begin to understand them. You'll understand their motives and their emotions. You'll be able to figure out what their actions will be – not just now, but into the future. Their actions will affect everything around them - including you, if you're involved with them. That will let you decide, is this someone you want to be involved with? How will their actions affect you? Will it be for the good, or will it be for the bad? Knowledge is power."

"This sounds so mystical."

"There is nothing mystical about it. All of these things I'm talking about have been studied. Body language is a well-established science. But, just like most of the sciences, people ignore it. It is all there for anyone to learn and use, but few people do. And, if you learn these ways, you can get people to give you almost anything you want. You can make business deals no one else can. And, you can get women to jump into your bed."

"Is that how you got your money?"

"Yes. People are always communicating their needs. If you understand what they're saying, you can give it to them. If you pay attention to people and see them, you'll know what they're thinking. Then, you can make deals with them. Give them what they want and they'll react in kind. Every relationship needs a leader. If you don't provide the leadership, they'll assume the role themselves. When that happens, you lose the advantage and the other person may not act in a responsible manner.

"Someone taught me the arts, now I'm passing them on to you – and a few others. The thing to remember, though, is how you use your skills will define who you are. Some people use them for selfish purposes, and their personalities and lives reflect it. Others aren't so greedy and they have much fuller lives. There is nothing wrong with profiting from your hard work, but it's wrong to take advantage of others. Like I said, your actions always start a series of events. The consequences of your actions will typically reflect the spirit of what you do. Act badly and the consequences will be bad. Act with a good spirit and the consequences will benefit those around you and, ultimately, benefit you."

She was trimming the lavender, smelling deeply of the flowers. He could peek down her blouse when she bent over and liked what he could see.

"Don't these smell wonderful?" she asked as she put them on the pile he was holding.

He smelled them and nodded in agreement. "Again, this all sounds mystical."

"The answer is still 'no.' Imagine you take advantage of people all the time. Who are you surrounded by? People who know you can't be trusted and treat you that way.

11

But, if you take care of people around you then the people around you will treat you accordingly. There's nothing mystical about that. It is simply a case of reaping what you sow. So, Roger, what kind of person are you going to be?" She stopped and smiled at him, waiting for his answer.

"You surprised me that time. I can't hide anything from you. You already know what kind of person I am, better than I know myself."

She gave a quiet laugh. "Yes, I know. You wouldn't be here if I hadn't known from the beginning. It wasn't an accident that you're here. I just want you to think about it for yourself."

Roger nodded, "I will. I promise."

"I'm going to see to it you keep your word. Come on. That's enough talking for today. Let's put these in vases. Then, there's a new position I want to show you in the bedroom before you need to go home. We don't want your parents to wonder where you've been."

Chapter Two

The harsh sunlight belied the fact that it was late December. Patricia's children, Greg and Chelsea, were on Christmas break and she liked to spend time with each of them individually. Yesterday, she had taken Chelsea out for an arts and crafts afternoon. Today, she decided to take Greg to Twin Lake, a small reservoir on the edge of town. They talked as they walked along the path, enjoying the cool, winter temperatures. The surface of the lake was calm and smooth and they could see the clouds reflected as if in a mirror.

"Mom, I heard you and Dad talking about a friend of yours. You said he's dying and you are going to do some stuff for him. Does that mean you'll be going away?"

Patricia was sorry he had heard, but glad he asked. "Yes, Roger Tucci. I'll probably have to spend time away from you kids and your father when he dies. I hope it won't be for a while, though."

"Why do you have to go away when he's the one that's dying?"

"Because he asked me to take care of his business. There are things that need to be taken care of and I don't know how much time I'll have to spend on it. He's made decisions about things and there's no telling what will happen because of that."

"I don't understand, Mom."

"Okay, let me put it this way. Look at the lake. The surface is all nice and smooth. Right?"

"Yeah."

Patricia picked up a stone and threw it. It hit the water with a splash, sending ripples out in all directions.

"What about now?" she asked him.

"There's ripples."

"So, I changed the lake. Roger's decisions are like those ripples. I don't know where they'll go, but I'll have to deal with them."

"But, in a little while the ripples will be gone and the lake will be smooth again. Why not just wait? Maybe things will go back to normal."

They stopped and sat on a bench where they could look over the water.

"That's right, the ripples will go away. But, the stone will still be in the lake. The lake will never be the same. And, those ripples will spread out over the lake. They will move things. They will cause a little bit of erosion. No matter what, the lake will never be the same again. Maybe the change will be big and unexpected. Maybe it will be small and expected. Either way, I did something to the lake and it will never be the same. That's what my friend has done. He's thrown stones out into the lake of life and no one knows what the ripples will do. It won't be for a while, yet. Maybe a couple months. But, when that day comes, I'll be the one who has to fix things."

"Why you?"

"Because he asked me to and I promised him I would."

"Couldn't the ripples have done something good?"

"Absolutely. In fact, good things don't just happen on their own. Someone has to make them happen. Generally, all of our actions are never all good or all bad. They will have some good consequences and they will have some bad. That's something we need to think about before we act. Just wonder, what will be the consequence of you and I spending this time together? Maybe if we had stayed in town we might have bought the winning lottery ticket. Or, maybe we would have both gotten hit by a car. We'll never know because we made the decision to come out here instead. And, that's the way of life."

Greg was thinking about what she had told him and, slowly, the lake surface became smooth again.

"I think I understand. You're saying your friend has done things and that has changed things for us."

"That's right. Those changes might be good, or they might be bad. It's hard to say. But, we always have to think about it before we act."

With that, she bent over and picked up a couple of rocks, handing one to her son.

"So, what do you want to do with it? If you throw it, it might cause good things and it might cause bad ones."

Greg bounced the stone in his hand, weighing it, before he dropped it to the ground.

"I don't want to decide."

14

Patricia nodded. "And, that's a decision, too," she said as she threw her stone out as far as she could, making a big splash in the water. Sometimes, you just need to have faith."

They stood up and she put her arm over his shoulder as, together, they walked away. Behind them, the ripples from her stone spread out over the lake.

§§§§§

Roger looked around his desk before going to the office door and asking his secretary, "Jana, have you seen the file with the conference account paperwork?"

Jana Genova came into his office with a bewildered look.

"What did you say?"

"I asked if you would get me the file on the conference account. Why? Is there a problem?"

"Fried eggs are blue and ride in train cars? Roger, what are you talking about?"

"What? Are you playing some kind of game?"

"Elephant trunks and rabbit ears? Roger, you're not making any sense."

"What do you mean I'm not making sense? I just want the paperwork file."

"Okay, Roger. You're scaring me," she said as she took him by the arm and led him back to his desk. "Listen to me. I don't think you know what you're saying. Please! Sit down. I'm calling the doctor."

She was just earnest enough to convince him to sit down.

"I'm fine. You don't need to call the doctor," he shouted after her.

What she heard was "Red rubber balls are good for badminton."

§§§§§

Dr. Takahashi shined a small light into Roger's eyes and quickly pulled it away, watching the reaction of Roger's pupils.

"How do you feel, Roger?"

"I told you, I feel fine."

15

"You told me you feel fine. Is that correct?"

"Yes! Why are you asking me a question like that?"

Dr. Takahashi sat back and put his pen light away.

"I wanted to make sure that what I heard was what you thought you were saying. Your secretary brought you in because you were speaking gibberish, but didn't realize it."

"You had a transient ischemic attack," he continued. "A mini-stroke. It's a temporary interruption of blood flow to the brain. The most common symptoms are weakness or numbness on one side of the body, slurred or garbled speech, impaired vision and dizziness. They normally last only a few minutes and don't cause permanent disability, but they are a warning you may have a full-fledged stroke in the future. Your gibberish was a symptom. You thought you were saying one thing, but there was a disconnect in your brain and you were actually saying something else. From your point of view, what you were saying made perfect sense. To anyone else it sounded like random words."

Roger was stunned by this development and Takahashi let him think for a few moments before asking, "Is this the first time? Have there been other instances?"

"Yes. I didn't realize it at the time, but now, looking back, there have been some other events. My left arm went all tingly the other day and I could barely lift anything with it. It went away after a few minutes and I didn't think anything more about it until now. There was also a time my vision was all screwy. Again, it only lasted a couple of minutes. I thought it might have been a side-effect of the medicine."

The doctor nodded and looked at Roger's charts.

"Your blood pressure is a little high, not real high, but it could stand to come down. I want to get you on some medication to treat it. It's the best I can do, considering your situation. But, Roger, you need to understand either a mini-stroke or a full stroke can occur at any time without warning. You need to consider this whenever you do something. You might want to think about not driving anymore, for instance. Don't climb anything tall, like a ladder."

"Is this an indicator we're entering the final stretch?"

"I don't know. It certainly means the disease is progressing."

16

Roger nodded his understanding. "You originally gave me maybe six months. It's been more than four now. I got to spend one more Christmas with my children, so I'm thankful."

Instead of returning to the office, Roger went home to think. He had put off dealing with things but the time had come to make some decisions. He poured himself a drink and sat in his favorite easy chair.

This was it. The end. Everyone knows the day is coming, but that's an abstract we all learn to deal with. This was no vague 'we all die' moment.

He had been putting off making plans. Patricia Kennealy had agreed to be the agent for his power of attorney but that was all he had done. Now, he began to mentally make a list of things he needed to do. There was paperwork for the business that needed to be straightened out for her. He needed to set up a brown book for her – a collection of passwords, bank accounts, insurance information, the location of his will – all of those things someone would need in order to take care of someone else's business.

Roger could only look around the room and wonder how many more times he was going to enjoy sitting here. He drank from the glass in his hand. It was getting more and more difficult to swallow and he wondered how many more times he would enjoy the taste of good whiskey. He thought of all the women he had known and wondered how many more times he would enjoy the company of a beautiful woman.

The last thought motivated him to retrieve his address book. Sitting back down, he sipped his drink as he went through the pages of contacts. Many of the names were business associates and some were friends. But, many were women he had known over the years. As the names marched through his memory he thought pleasant thoughts and smiled. Each of the women had a special place in his heart, but one name stood out as he flipped the pages. He thought about how she hadn't been the brightest of women, but boy, she sure knew her way around the bedroom. They had met while he was in college and he thought at one time she was 'the one.' He pulled out his phone and dialed the number he had written down, hoping it was still good.

"Sharon? Hi! It's Roger Tucci. I was just sitting here thinking about you and decided to give you a call. How're you doing? Good, I'm glad to hear it. I'm doing fine, too. No, I'm still in Dallas. Where are you, still in Idaho Falls? Yes, I remember. Listen,

I'm taking some time off to travel around and I was going to be in your area. I would love to see you again. Really? That would be great. I'll check, but I should be in Idaho tomorrow, will that work? Wonderful! I'll call back with the details. Good. Me, too. Bye."

After hanging up, he got on the computer and bought a plane ticket to Idaho Falls. If you have to go, he thought, you might as well go out in style.

§§§§§

It had been a wild weekend. For three days they didn't even leave the house, opting for delivery instead of cooking their meals or going out. They were so involved with what they were doing he even missed his flight back home. It seemed as if they were trying to set a new land-speed record for the bedroom.

Until the stroke.

They had just finished making love when Roger complained about a sudden headache. Getting up to get some water, he took a few steps across the room before collapsing without warning in convulsions and vomiting. Sharon panicked and didn't know what to do. Through sheer ignorant luck, she ended up doing the correct thing by dialing 911. It saved Roger's life. For a while, at least.

§§§§§

Patricia got the call late that night and woke John to tell him the news.

"They said the stroke was massive. Roger suffered a lot of brain damage," she said quietly. "He can't make decisions for himself anymore. That means the power of attorney provisions have kicked in. I have to make decisions for him now."

John sat up in the bed and rubbed his face to help wake himself up.

"Alright. What are you going to do?"

"He's in Idaho, so I have to go up there."

"Idaho? What in the world is he doing up there?"

"I'm not sure of the details, but it sounds like he went up to see an old girlfriend."

18

John shook his head in amazement. "The guy is about to drop dead and all he can think of is getting laid?"

She lay down by her husband before answering, "It's what Tiggers do best."

John chuckled at her joke. "When are you leaving?"

"Tomorrow, if I can get a flight."

"How long do you think you'll be gone?"

"A couple of days. I need to check with the doctors to learn what condition he's in before I make any decisions."

He kissed her on the top of her head. "Don't worry. Go take care of Roger. I'll call the nursery and explain things to them. I'll take care of the kids."

"You?"

"What? You don't think men have a nurturing side?"

"Sure, you do. You just don't know where you put it down half the time."

"Trust me, I'll take good care of them."

"You haven't been paying attention lately, have you? They're about grown up. It's more likely they'll take care of you."

§§§§§

As Patricia made her way down the hospital hallway, she could hear the disturbing sounds of a man screaming in pain. It wasn't until she approached the ward they had directed her to that she realized it was Roger doing the screaming.

The sights and sounds as she entered the open ward stunned her and all she could do was stand and watch in numb silence while the nurses tried to restrain Roger as he was thrashing in pain. One of them finally realized she was standing there.

"You can't be here. You have to get out."

The nurse's challenge finally broke her trance. "What is going on here? What are you doing to him?"

"Ma'am! You aren't allowed in here. You have to leave now!"

"No, I'm his power-of-attorney agent so I have every right to be here."

"Ma'am, if you don't leave now I will call security."

19

Patricia was getting angrier by the second. She turned her gaze from Roger to look at the nurse and the woman realized right away she didn't want to deal with Patricia.

"Fine," Patricia told her in a level voice, "I think that's a good idea. Please call security. And, I would like to know where his doctor is, too."

The nurse left quickly to make the phone calls. As she left, Patricia pulled out her cell phone and made a video recording of Roger screaming in his bed while the one nurse tried to finish restraining him. Soon, the nurse who had left returned with a security guard.

"Ma'am. I have to ask you to leave! Please put the phone down right now!"

Patricia turned off the video and began working with the phone as she told the guard, "I am this man's legal guardian. I have court documents in my purse that say so. That means I have every right to be here. If you try to make me leave I'll sue the crap out of this hospital. Do you really want to take that responsibility?"

The guard hesitated. He wasn't paid to make those kinds of decisions. But, he couldn't let her record what was going on. He got his radio out to make a call.

"I'm calling my supervisor. Meanwhile, I need you to give me that phone. You can't be recording events inside the hospital."

"Would you like to take it from me by force?" she asked as she continued to play with it. "Besides, I just sent that video to the cloud and emailed it to half a dozen people. If you want, I can post it on Facebook and send it out on Twitter."

The guard hesitated.

"I didn't think so. Get your supervisor here and I want to see Mr. Tucci's doctor right away."

The guard decided it was best to retreat and left while making some calls on his radio. It didn't take long for him to return with his supervisor.

"Ma'am. I'm going to have to ask you to leave," the supervisor said. "If you don't leave right away you'll be arrested."

Patricia merely handed him the legal documents she was holding. "Any questions?" she asked. "Now, I'll say it one more time. I want to see Mr. Tucci's doctor and I mean right now! You want to talk about someone being arrested? How about I call the police and inform them of what's going on here? Denying a patient his required medical care and causing undue suffering has to be against some law. And, I'll call up the local news stations, too. Won't that look good on the evening news? You better consult with your legal people before you even *THINK* of putting a hand on me! Do you *UNDERSTAND* me?" Her eyes and nostrils were flaring as she dressed down the security man. "Now, give me my papers back and go get the *DOCTOR!*"

At that moment a doctor came into the ward, "What's going on here? Who's this woman and why haven't you removed her?"

Patricia answered for the security people. "I'll tell you who I am. I'm Mr. Tucci's legal guardian and I'm here to look after his best interests. Now, I want to know why you're not giving him anything for his pain? *LOOK AT HIM!*" She thrust her arm out in Roger's direction. As she was talking, the two security people decided this was a good opportunity to leave. Now it was just her, the doctor and the two nurses, and the nurses were trying to melt away. Patricia's anger had been increasing while she was waiting and she had nearly reached the point of exploding. Now, she had someone to take it out on and that was what she planned on doing. As she talked, she kept stepping towards the doctor, forcing him to back up before the onslaught and they were soon in the corridor.

"I asked you a question! Why aren't you giving him anything for the pain?"

The nurses were busy clearing people out of the hallway so the two of them were alone. The doctor finally regained his composure enough to answer her.

"We're doing everything we can. We're trying to treat his pain, but we're having a difficult time getting the dosage right."

"Then, why not give him something stronger?"

"We can only do what is covered, and his insurance company has said they won't cover him."

"*WHAT?!!!* You're letting him scream in pain while you fight it out with the insurance company? What kind of sick bastard are you?"

At this point the head nurse came up and asked them, "Would you like to go into the office to discuss this?" Patricia and the doctor simultaneously turned to her and angrily shouted, "No! We're fine!"

Patricia leveled a deadly gaze at the doctor. "This is what you're going to do. You're going to go in there right now and give him whatever it takes to deaden the pain.

If you don't, I'll broadcast it to every news channel and media outlet I can find. Then, we'll talk."

The doctor locked his gaze with her and was about to argue before he thought better of it. Pushing his way past her, he called for the nurse and headed for Roger's beside.

"Get me the morphine," he told her.

Patricia watched as the doctor administered the injection. Roger began to settle down very quickly and within a few minutes had fallen into a deep sleep.

Once she was satisfied Roger had been taken care of, she leveled her gaze at the doctor and said, "Now, you're going to tell me everything that has been going on."

§§§§§

After talking with Dr. Seabolt, she found a quiet place to sit without being disturbed and collected her thoughts before calling her husband.

"How are you doing," he asked. "Are you handling it okay?"

"Not really. It's been tough. After knowing him for so long it's heart-breaking to see him like this. It just seems so unfair."

"I know. I'm here for you."

The words almost made her choke up. "Thank you."

"How long do you think you'll be there?"

"A couple of days. There's some paperwork I need to take care of and I don't trust this hospital to do the right thing without someone around to watch them."

"Why? What's wrong?"

"He was screaming in pain when I arrived and they wouldn't give him anything strong enough to deal with it until I made them."

"Why in the world wouldn't they treat his pain?"

"Money. The insurance company won't cover him. They told the hospital he only has coverage in Texas and it doesn't extend to Idaho."

"You've got to kidding me! They're going to let someone in their hospital suffer because the insurance company won't pony up?"

22

"Believe me, we had it out and I've done as much as I can."

Even with the grim news, Patricia's comment made John chuckle. "Yeah, I bet you did. The red-headed fireball. Those guys probably have no idea what hit them."

"John, there's more. The stroke was so massive he has suffered serious brain damage," she told him. "The cancer has gotten seriously worse. He doesn't have long to live."

"I'm sorry. How's he doing?"

"He's asleep right now. But John, Roger has a living will and the terms are very clear – there are to be no extraordinary measures to prolong his life."

"Okay. So, what does that mean?"

"He's on life-support. I have to pull the plug."

§§§§§

Dr. Seabolt met with the administrator, Haywood Alban, about Roger after Patricia left. He was reading a copy of the power-of-attorney Patricia had provided them.

"What are his chances," Alban asked.

"Well, he doesn't have any chance at all. I told her he's terminal and is only being kept alive with life support. He has a living will and she's going to unplug him. I'm not sure how long he'll live, but it can't be very long. We're talking days, not weeks."

"What about this woman? Any chance she might do something?"

"The only thing she could do that would be any trouble would be to take him back to Texas," the doctor told him.

"If she gets him back there alive, then he'll be covered by the insurance company." Alban held up the document he was holding. "We want him to die before she can get him back. If he is as sick as you say, what are the chances he survives the trip?"

"He would never survive a car trip. The stress would almost certainly kill him within even a few hours. He might survive a plane trip, but I don't think any airline would let him fly."

The administrator nodded in understanding. "I don't think we need to tell her of the risks involved. It would be good if we could get her to take him off our hands. If he

23

dies in her custody it isn't our fault." He sighed and leaned back in his chair. "Well, if we get lucky, he'll die quickly and this whole problem will go away."

Interlude

Trudi Legrande wasn't a particularly attractive woman, by most standards. She was what people generously called 'big-boned' and 'manly.' Less generous people would never hide their thoughts – or their jokes. They would outline a fat person with their hands as they joked "Truly, le grande," as if they thought they were being clever. Men she met all felt they deserved someone more attractive, someone better. She had come to accept it as her lot in life. Working the service desk at the car repair, she knew, was her fate.

The mechanics would work a report up on the vehicles brought in for servicing and send it to her. She would then page the customer and brief them before either getting their approval on an estimate or taking payment if the job was completed. She made up for her lack of a love life by being the hardest worker in the office. As a result, the other workers learned they could leave her by herself while they took a break together. She was the only one there when the report came across the counter for a car towed in that morning.

Roger Tucci was just one more customer, albeit a very good-looking one. In her most professional manner, she went over the mechanic's report with him. The problem was he wasn't looking at the report as she discussed it. He was looking at her. In fact, he was looking at her so intently she thought it should make her uncomfortable. Instead, she found herself falling into his eyes.

Pulling herself back to reality, she asked, "Mr. Tucci, are you paying attention?"

"Yes, my dear. I've heard every word. I have a rental car waiting for me. You know you are a very beautiful woman. Your husband is a lucky man."

"I don't have a husband," she blurted before she realized what she was saying.

"My apologies, your boyfriend then."

She blushed slightly as she replied, "No boyfriend, either." *What I am doing?* she thought. Why was she telling this total stranger about her personal life? Why did she feel so comfortable talking to him?

"Look, Mr. Tucci. I need your approval on this estimate before they can begin work. You understand, it will take a few days to complete the repair?"

25

"Yes, I understand," he said as he signed where she indicated. "That means I have more time to see you. Would you care to have dinner with me tonight? It would be my pleasure. Please say yes."

Everything told her to say no, but when she looked into that gorgeous face she couldn't help herself.

"Well, I wasn't planning anything this evening. Only dinner, though."

"Absolutely. I'm stranded here in town until my car gets fixed and a little friendly company would be wonderful." He held his hand out and said, "Call me Roger."

"Okay, Roger. I'm Trudi."

Roger looked at her name tag and said, "Trudi Lagrande." Out of reflex, Trudi braced herself for the inevitable joke. "The 'great strength,'" he said. "I can see that in you. Beautiful and with a great strength. Your parents named you well. Let me give you my number. I'll be staying in the Sheraton. Give me a call when you get off work and I'll pick you up. I am looking forward to it."

She stood there surprised with her own behavior. When her coworkers returned from their break they didn't even notice the way she was smiling.

Her supervisor the next morning noticed when she came in late. This had never happened before. She was usually the first one to arrive every day.

"Trudi! Why are you late?"

She had been ready with a made-up story to tell him, but instead found herself saying, "I was making love."

Her answer was so unexpected, he didn't know how to react and settled for an admonishment. "Please keep your personal life to yourself. And, don't do it again," he told her as he walked off.

"No, sir." But she thought to herself, "*Oh, I'm going to do him as much as I can.*"

For three days Trudi lived a life of which she had only dreamed. Roger treated her better than she had ever been treated and not only told her she was beautiful, but made her feel it. She was sorry to see him go, but not heartbroken. She never had any illusions about the tryst. It was wonderful, but not forever.

Instead, she bought herself a new wardrobe, got her hair done and learned how to apply make-up. Her coworkers couldn't help but notice the difference and some of them

26

felt resentful to see the simple girl turning into a beautiful woman as they watched. One of them vented her resentment one day when, indicating Trudi's new dress, she made the familiar fat-person motion and said, "Truly, le grande!"

Trudi turned on her and angrily said, "I don't know why you would think that was an appropriate comment. I don't want to ever hear you saying something like that again!"

Everyone who witnessed it couldn't believe the change in Trudi. This was a different person than the one they had learned to take advantage of.

Trudi started dating and it wasn't long before she found a man she was very happy with. He told her the thing that first attracted him to her was the way she radiated an inner beauty. When they got married, she left the auto shop with no regrets. She never mentioned the man who taught her how to be beautiful. But, she never forgot him, either.

Chapter Three

When Patricia arrived at the hospital the next morning there was a tall, blonde woman waiting for her. In her 30s, this woman was dressed in a button-down expensive business suit and her hair was perfectly coifed. She carried herself with unbending professionalism.

"Mrs. Kennealy, I'm Fredericka Boroughs. If you'll come this way I can answer all of your questions concerning Mr. Tucci." She showed Patricia to her office and took a seat behind a large, wooden desk. The office smelled of fresh coffee.

"Mrs. Kennealy, let me begin by saying how sorry I am about the condition of your friend and the way he has been treated while in Northern Bonneville Hospital. Understand, we are a private, for-profit hospital and we have to manage our costs very closely. In fact, Mr. Tucci should never have been brought here at all. That was a mistake on the part of the emergency service personnel."

"So, what you're saying is you don't allow people that can't afford you."

"No, that isn't our policy. It's just that we administer to private customers and are not a public institution."

"You just deny patients needed medication in order to save money."

The representative shook her head as she answered, "It was very unfortunate and is not the policy of this hospital. The individuals involved will be dealt with, I assure you. And, I also want to make sure you know Mr. Tucci will receive all of the care he needs from now on."

"Thank you. I'm grateful for that and I know Mr. Tucci is, as well."

"We obviously made a bad impression on you and we just want to change that. Along those lines, I need to discuss Mr. Tucci's condition with you. You have already indicated you will be discontinuing life support in accordance with his living will, correct?"

"Yes, that's correct. I have no choice in the matter."

"I understand and I'm not trying to change your mind. We will assist you in whatever manner we can. I am sympathetic to how difficult this is. All you have to do is ask if there is anything that isn't to your satisfaction."

"Thank you. I have to ask, if Roger is such a burden on your hospital, why haven't you moved him?"

"I'm glad you asked. The fact is, we tried. We contacted area hospitals and assisted living facilities and none of them would take him without insurance coverage. The law says we have to take care of him until we can find somewhere else for him to go. For that reason, I would like to talk to you about his future. Since you're his legal guardian, these decisions are yours now."

"What do you mean by 'his future'?"

"We would like to have him leave the hospital." Boroughs opened a file she had on her desk and put several papers in front of Patricia. "These are the release forms for you to take Mr. Tucci out of the hospital and return him to Dallas. We are prepared to help you anyway we can. It isn't likely you can fly him back, so you would have to drive him back in a van so he can lie down. We are willing to let you have one of our old gurneys. It can be modified to allow it to be strapped to the floor in the back. We will provide you with the necessary supplies, including all medication, that you would need. We will even give you the training so you can administer his IV and injections. It would only take a few minutes."

"Wait a minute! Are you kicking him out of your hospital?"

"I just told you, we can't do that. But, as his legal guardian, you can take him to another facility, if you would agree to that."

"I can't believe you people."

"Please, ma'am, I already explained. We are a private hospital administering to a private clientele. By receiving treatment without insurance coverage, Mr. Tucci is causing the cost of medical coverage to go up for our regular clients. That isn't fair to them."

"Fair? I really don't care what is fair to your rich clients. Roger is here and you need to provide him with whatever medical care he needs."

"We understand that and that won't be a problem." She slid another document in front of Patricia. "In the case Mr. Tucci stays here, we would like you to sign this agreement that the hospital can bill his estate for whatever expenses we can't recoup from the insurance company."

"I'll tell you what, I'll take these documents with me and have my lawyer look them over."

"Please understand, these offers are only good for today. If you feel you need to take more time to decide, we will not be obliged to honor them."

"That's fine. I'll take that chance. I'm not sure I heard any kind of deal anyway," she said as she folded the documents and put them in her purse. "Now, I would like to go spend some private time with Roger. This isn't easy for me, even if I have no choice."

"Certainly. Would you like me to take you there?"

"No, I know the way and I think I would rather be alone right now."

"I understand. Just one last question. Do you mind if I ask a personal question?" Patricia didn't know how to react and hesitated before responding that it would be okay. "We were wondering, just who are you? Are you the girlfriend?"

"No, I'm nothing more than an old friend Roger asked to help out."

"Well, that helps. There's a woman here claiming to be the girlfriend and demanding to see Mr. Tucci. We've been able to put her off, so far."

The tall blonde rose, indicating the meeting was over.

"And, I hope you understand we aren't being some kind of cruel, heartless business. We have clients that trust us to take care of their best interests. I'm sure you would feel the same way if you were one of our clients."

"Ms. Boroughs, I don't think I would ever feel the same way as you. The thought of a hospital rejecting patients because they might cut into its profits kind of makes me sick to my stomach. I hope you can live with yourself."

Patricia spent the time walking to where she had seen Roger the day before calming herself and collecting her thoughts. She didn't want to be upset when she saw him. By the time she got there, she was able to produce a fake smile and felt calm enough to speak without showing her anger. As she entered the room, she found a woman straddling Roger and lifting her skirt up. The scene was so preposterous it took Patricia a moment to understand what was happening. But, then she erupted.

"What are you doing?! Oh, my god! Are you trying to have sex with him?"

The startled woman quickly got down, smoothing her skirt in the process.

"What the hell are you thinking?"

The woman held out her hand and said, "Hi! I'm Sharon. I'm Roger's friend. I was just checking on him."

"Checking on him? With your panties on the floor?" Patricia pointed to the pair of panties lying next to Roger's bed.

"What? Oh, no. Those aren't mine. They must be some else's. Maybe one of the nurses, or someone. Listen, I need to get going. It was nice meeting you."

With that, she quickly grabbed the panties and hurried out of the room, leaving Patricia in a dazed state of bewilderment.

"I can't frigging believe it! The guy is dying in a hospital bed and he's still getting laid!"

§§§§§

Roger was awake, but drugged and unable to talk because of the respirator in his mouth. He was able to signal to Patricia as she sat with him through the rest of the morning, talking to him and reading emails from friends sending their condolences. Finally, she fell quiet and sat with her head down. Her hand rested on the bed, feeling the cool sheets. Roger, gently squeezing her hand, brought her back from her thoughts.

"I'm sorry, Roger. I know what I have to do, but I don't want to."

He lightly patted her and weakly nodded to her.

"Oh, Roger. What am I supposed to do?"

He gave his shoulders a light shrug and tilted his head.

"Yes, I know. Get rid of the options you can't do and the decision is much easier. Well, not this time. The decision has been made and it's not in my hands. That doesn't make it easier, though."

He gave her hand another soft squeeze, then left his hand resting on hers. She sat silently, thinking of what was to come. Roger's breathing got calmer and she realized he had fallen asleep. The morphine, she knew, meant his sleep was very deep. Keeping her hand under his, she was able to reach the call button with her other hand to summon the nurse. When she arrived, Patricia turned to her and said, "Would you call the doctor, please? I think we're ready."

She was still silently sitting in the same position when the nurse returned with the doctor.

"I understand you want to take the patient off life support. Is that right?"

"His name is Roger Tucci. And, no, I don't want to take him off, but it's his wish. I have filled out and signed the documents and turned them over to Ms. Boroughs. He's asleep. This is as good a time as any. Please do what needs to be done."

The doctor nodded his understanding and proceeded to remove all of the equipment keeping Roger's body alive. When he was done, Roger looked as if he had simply dozed off. The monitoring equipment was still attached and Patricia watched the readouts, expecting them to flatline, but they didn't. The doctor examined them for several seconds before giving his assessment.

"His vitals are still quite strong, considering his condition. I can't tell you how long he will remain alive, but there is nothing here to indicate his demise is imminent."

He continued to watch the readouts for several minutes.

"Yes, his vitals are steady. I think he's safe for now. He might even last a few weeks. It's impossible to say with any certainty."

"But, the end is coming?"

"Yes. I'm afraid there is nothing that can be done about that."

"Will he wake up?"

"I don't know. It's possible. If he does, his waking periods will get shorter and less frequent. Of course, remember he is on heavy medication. He may have hallucinations when he's awake."

"I understand. Thank you, doctor."

The doctor nodded and left Patricia to be alone with her friend.

§§§§§

Patricia turned her phone on when she took a break from the ward and saw she had a text message from Roger's secretary, Jana Genova. It said she had Roger's financial statements and asked Patricia to call when she could.

"Hi, Jana? This is Patricia. What do you have?"

33

"I have Roger's financials, just like you asked. I had his accountant go through all of his bank accounts and check into all of his assets and all of that stuff." Patricia didn't like the sound of anxiety in the secretary's voice but let her continue. "He gave me a big statement and I don't understand most of it."

"It's okay, Jana. I just need a quick summary. How much money does Roger have to cover his expenses?"

"None. He doesn't have any money."

Patricia was stunned by what she had heard. "None? Nothing? You're telling me he has no money at all?"

"Well, he does have $63, but that's it."

"$63? How is that possible? He made millions of dollars over the years. Where did it all go?"

"I don't know. I'm as surprised as you are. Patricia, I'm scared. How am I going to get paid if he doesn't have any money? I have bills to pay. What am I supposed to do?"

"Stay calm," she said. "I'll need some time to look things over. Have the accountant send me the records so I can get an idea of what's going on. And, Jana? Could you get Roger's medical insurance policy for me? I need to contact the insurance company."

"I have his insurance information right here. The hospital has been in touch with me. Patricia, I know you want to be there for Roger, but we need someone here to run things. You're the only one that can make decisions now. The company is in debt. Tens of thousands of dollars in debt. You need to come home. Things are coming apart and you're the only one who has authority to keep them together."

"Jana, Roger might die any moment. I don't want to leave him alone."

"We can get someone else to be with him. I know you want to be there, but we really need you here."

Patricia hesitated for a moment. She did want to stay with Roger. He might die at any moment. But, Jana was right. She had responsibilities now. Roger wasn't the only one depending on her.

"Okay. I'm on my way as soon as I can get a flight."

"I already checked. There's a flight this morning. You can still catch it and be in Dallas early in the afternoon."

"All right. Book me on that flight. I'm going to say good-bye to Roger and I'll be on my way."

After ending the call, she sat dazed for a few minutes as she thought about this new situation before muttering, "What am I going to do now?"

Interlude

Roger had wanted to drop out of school and use his newfound observational skills to make a living, but his muse wouldn't let him. Instead, she made him promise to not only finish high school but to go on to college.

"Education isn't a panacea, but it's the closest thing you're going to find. You have worked hard at observing things around you and you're getting good, but you also need to know how to put them to good use. There is much more to learn at a university than the stuff they'll teach you from books. Pay attention to what's going on around you."

As a result, Roger enrolled at the University of Texas, majoring in business. His parents weren't well off, but they were able to put together the money needed to pay his expenses, and he appreciated the sacrifice they made for him.

It didn't take long to realize just how much there was to learn in a university setting. Being in such a busy environment gave him an opportunity to practice his observational skills on a much greater variety of people than he ever could before. He was able to influence his teachers in ways the other students could only fantasize about. He was able to make contacts he expected to help him in future business deals. And, the constant flow of female companionship to help pass the lonely evenings away from home was better than anything he could have imagined.

Life at UT was good.

In the spring of his second year at UT, Roger took advantage of the weather to walk to a local diner he enjoyed for lunch. He was relaxing after his meal, doing his observation routine and trying to decide how he was going to spend the rest of the day, when he noticed a man come in and take a seat at a table across the room from him. With years of practice behind him, Roger was able to determine much about the man with very little effort. Roger knew he was a blue-collar man by the fact he was dressed in worn, but clean working clothes and carried himself with the swagger of someone confident in his ability to work hard. The man was clearly aggravated though, indicating to Roger something wasn't going well. He kept touching his pocket with his wallet in it, suggesting money was an issue. He was flipping through a small notebook, probably looking for contact information, but he wasn't finding what he needed. And, he would look apprehensively out the restaurant window. His straw cowboy hat sat on the chair next to him, but he kept wiping at his forehead anyway. Despite the man's self-confidence, Roger could see he was worried about something.

As Roger was going through his list of observations, it dawned on him – this guy was desperate to make a deal. Suddenly, Roger was intrigued and decided to introduce himself.

"Hi, there mister," Roger said as he extended his hand. "My name's Roger Tucci. How are you doing today?" Roger had already figured out the man wasn't doing very well at all and wanted to coax his story out of him.

"Hi, son. Virgil Wenner," he said, taking Roger's hand. "I'm afraid I'm having a piss-poor day of it."

"I'm sorry to hear that. What's wrong?"

"I've got a load of venison in my truck and the man I was selling it to backed out. Now, I'm stuck with this load and don't know what to do with it. I've been calling around to find a buyer but with no luck. Now, I'm just hoping to find someone to offer a fire sale."

"I thought it was illegal to sell venison."

"Deer is illegal, but antelope is legal."

"Where do you get antelope meat?"

"From exotic game ranches."

"What's an exotic game ranch?"

"It's a ranch that stocks animals from other countries, mostly Africa. Since they aren't native species, there's no hunting season. Hunters pay big money to hunt at one of these places. If the herds get too large, they have to thin them out or the animals will overgraze. I buy the extras from a whole series of ranches and sell the meat. It's real tasty and a lot healthier than beef. It can even be kosher. Someday, there will be a big market for this meat. But right now, I have to sell it on individual contracts. That's what I had, but like I said, the guy changed his mind and decided he didn't have any need for a truckload of antelope meat. I could sue, but that won't help me much. I would just like to find a buyer so I can get on with my business."

37

"Really? How much do you want for it?"

"This load?" Virgil shook his head as he thought about it. "The deal I had was for $10,000 for the whole load, but now I would be happy to get even half that. I'd about break even, maybe lose a little, but it would be better than losing everything."

"Is that a fair price, $10,000?"

"It's about market. I might be able to get better if I wanted to wait and haggle, but time is money, as they say."

"Would you take $7,500 for it?"

"Son, if you could give me $7,500 I'd be your friend for life."

"How about being a regular supplier? How would you like to do this on a regular basis? How often could you deliver a truckload at $7,500 per load?"

Virgil had been too wrapped up in his troubles to pay much attention to Roger before. Now, he took a closer look at the young man dressed in slacks and a purple shirt. His dark hair and moustache complemented his youthful good looks and gave him a welcoming appearance. Even though he was young, there was something about Roger that made Virgil comfortable dealing with him.

"You're serious, aren't you?"

"Completely."

"What did you say your name was?"

"Roger. Roger Tucci."

"Well, Roger. If you think you can handle the business, I can deliver a truck load like this every three months. And, if I could be sure I'd have a firm price in advance, I'd agree to $7,500 per load. How's that sound?"

"It sounds good. Give me 30 minutes and I'll be right back."

"Okay, you've got 30 minutes, but no more. I need to move this load."

Roger located a phone book and started searching the listings. It took some work and a number of phone calls, but he finally found what he needed – the phone number for someone who needed to make a deal.

Alfred Prater ran a number of moderately successful restaurants catering to the semi-hippie crowd of Austin. Roger ate there frequently and realized Prater's business

38

was dropping. Alfred needed something different to set himself apart from the pack and Roger had an idea of what it could be.

"What if I told you I have a truckload of antelope venison? I can deliver it today for $8500 – better than fair market. It's a lot healthier than beef and real tasty. You would be the only restaurant in town offering healthy venison as a menu option. Would you be interested?" Roger asked him.

"Is this some kind of a joke?"

"No, not at all. And, I can deliver another truckload every three months. How's that sound?"

Prater thought it over. He had gotten where he was by recognizing when to take a calculated gamble. The truth was, business had been slowly going down for quite a while. He knew you had to keep producing a new product or the customers would drift away. This, he thought, might be the very thing he needed.

"It sounds like you just made my day, mister. How do you want to handle this?"

"Tell me where to deliver the meat and I'll be there in less than an hour. Have the cash ready and it's yours."

"This is all legal, isn't it? You're not selling me poached meat are you?"

"It's all legitimate. I'll have the papers to prove it. Plus, I want to do repeat business, remember?"

"Well, I'll still want to inspect everything, but I'll have the money ready."

Roger wrote down the address and hung up. An hour later, Alfred Prater was taking possession of a truckload of frozen venison, Virgil Wenner happily put $7,500 in his pocket before heading home with an empty truck, and Roger was $1,000 richer. For a college student in 1970, it was a good profit. It was his first business deal and he was feeling pretty satisfied. That evening, he called his parents and told them he had found a way to pay for his college education and they would not need to make the sacrifice anymore.

Initially, Roger ran the fledgling company from his dorm room, finding various suppliers who wanted a sure market for their products and buyers who didn't want to sign contracts obligating them to purchase anything. He would take the deliveries and find customers who needed the load quickly. Seldom did he ever need to store anything for more than a day or two. As he added customers and clients, he made enough money to rent an office and hire some employees. Within a year, it was a secure business, but one which Roger had no interest in running. So he sold it for a handsome profit.

Roger couldn't help but be amazed. All he did was to recognize someone's need and then find a way to satisfy it, making more money than he ever had before in the process.

Roger had found his business model.

Chapter Four

"I'm sorry, Mrs. Kennealy, but the decision is pretty simple. The hospital says Mr. Tucci created this situation himself and if he dies from it they will classify it as a suicide. In that case, the insurance company has no recourse but to deny any claim against his policy."

"Suicide?! You can't commit suicide by stroke!"

"He knew what his medical condition was. He was having mini-strokes and he took himself out of his doctor's care to go away for a weekend of sex. His conduct was reckless, irresponsible and self-inflicted. That qualifies as suicide."

"This is insane! What if he had stayed in Dallas for a weekend of wild sex and had the stroke?"

"He would have still been in the care of his doctor, so he would have been covered. It isn't the wild sex that's the problem."

"What you're telling me is, the key point is that he left his doctor's care?"

"Yes, if he had been with his doctor then it is assumed he was getting valid medical advice and care. When he left the state like that it says he had rejected the medical advice and chose to put himself in a situation he knew was likely to be harmful."

"We wouldn't be having this conversation if you would cover his medical care."

"When he left Texas we were no longer responsible for him. That is clearly spelled out in the coverage and Mr. Tucci signed off that he understood it."

"Why didn't they tell me this when I was in Idaho? Why am I finding out about this now? You guys have created a neat little system. Your company refuses to pay for his coverage and, since he doesn't have coverage, the hospital says it was a reckless act and is suicide, letting you guys completely off the hook. You take his premiums for years and then you won't deliver on your end of the deal."

"I'm sorry for his death, Mrs. Kennealy, but I'm just telling you what the contract says. I'm powerless to do anything else."

"Well, he's not dead yet. What if he returns to his doctor's care? Doesn't that prove he had no intention of rejecting the medical advice or doing anything harmful to himself?"

"Returning to his doctor's care would certainly remove that obstacle. But, I'm under the impression he can't travel."

"I'll talk to him and his doctor and we'll work something out. Until then, don't close out that claim."

"Of course, not. As long as he's alive he's one of our customers and will be treated accordingly."

Patricia hung up the phone and put her head in her hands before saying, "Oh, crap!"

§§§§§

As soon as Patricia collected herself, her next call was to Fredericka Boroughs at Northern Bonneville Hospital. She didn't waste time on small talk.

"What is this business about saying Roger Tucci is committing suicide? And, why didn't anyone tell me about this when I was up there?"

"I'm sorry you are upset. But, I did tell you and it's right there in the documents you signed. It says his condition is 'self-imposed.' And the fact is he brought this on himself."

"What are you talking about? How can you say a stroke is 'self-imposed'? Where are you getting the idea you can blame him for this?"

"His doctor in Dallas said he has been having mini-strokes and advised Mr. Tucci of the same. And yet, Mr. Tucci came up to Idaho, where he knew he had no insurance coverage, to have a weekend fling with an old girlfriend. He knew he was acting irresponsibly and in a manner that was likely to result in injury, even death."

It was hard to say she was wrong, so Patricia said nothing. Fredericka continued.

"Because of that, we have told the insurance company his condition is self-inflicted. Until he returns to his doctor's care, he is considered to be self-administrating and they won't cover his expenses."

"And, just how does the hospital expect to recoup its expenses? If you tell the insurance company it's suicide, they won't pay you. What do you have to gain by this?"

"I don't know the answer to that question. Those decisions are made by the administration, not me."

"Why are you telling me this?"

"I'm just trying to help. We discussed this already. If you can get him back to his doctor in Dallas the insurance company will cover him. We are prepared to assist you. He would have to be driven back. No airline will allow him to fly in the condition he's in, so it would need to be a van so he can lie down. We can adapt an old gurney so it can be strapped down and Mr. Tucci will be comfortable. We will give you the necessary supplies, including morphine, and we will train you on how to administer an IV and injections. That will take only a few minutes. Then, you can return Mr. Tucci to Dallas where he will be covered by his insurance."

"Very well. Give me a little time to sort things out. This is all unexpected."

"Of course. You have my number."

After ending the call, Fredericka sat back in her chair and, with a sigh, said to herself, "Well, I played my part."

§§§§§

"It's simple. The reason the hospital wants to classify it as suicide is all about money. If they call it a natural event, they will only get paid what the insurance company is willing to pay. We already know that won't be much since he's out of state, but anything will be enough. The insurance company will pay something rather than go to court. Roger's estate will be covered and there isn't much they can do about it."

Stan Woosley was about as cowboy as you could expect to find. His white, wide-brimmed straw hat hung from the horns of a longhorn steer on the wall above his head. Patricia knew that rack wasn't something he bought in a store. He raised the big animals on his ranch. He pulled open the lower drawer of his desk so he could prop his broken-in old boot on it. The surface of the drawer was scuffed up from the repeated abuse. Anyone thinking that meant he wasn't a good lawyer usually learned differently, sometimes to their sorrow. A graduate of the Baylor Law School, the oldest school of law in Texas, he had returned home to practice where the lifestyle was slow and peaceful. His dark hair

43

had turned salt and pepper with the years and his thick mustache was solid gray. His hair and the lines in his face testified to how long he had been in practice.

As Patricia listened intently, she hoped Stan would provide her with a way out of the mess she was in. She was very suspicious after her most recent conversation with Fredericka Boroughs and wondered why the hospital had suddenly become so helpful. After they ended the call, she had driven straight back to Cisco to get legal advice.

Stan continued, "But, if they classify it as suicide the insurance company will reject the claim and the estate expenses won't be covered. That gives the hospital permission to go after the estate for anything that is owed, including legal expenses and interest."

"But, Stan, the estate is broke. Roger didn't have any money left. There was $63 in his checking account and that's it. And, the company is heavily in debt. He didn't even have the money to pay his monthly rent. I don't know what he was thinking."

"He wasn't thinking. The cancer and the drugs were interfering with his ability to make rational decisions. The bad news is you are his estate. All of his creditors can come after you, including the hospital."

"What are you talking about? I merely agreed to clean up his affairs for him."

"No, you agreed to assume full responsibility for his estate. It's right here in the power-of-attorney document. That means you not only have the full legal authority to make decisions in his name, but you took on the responsibility as well. I wish you had consulted with me before you did this. I would have warned you."

The walls started closing in and Patricia thought she was about to black out.

"Stan, it could be hundreds of thousands of dollars."

"It already is. I checked after you called. His hospital bill by itself is over a hundred thousand. Private for-profit hospitals charge up to ten times the accepted Medicare/Medicaid rates. The very best they will get from the insurance company is the accepted rate. They want to come after the estate rather than take what the insurance company will offer. I'm assuming you provided the hospital a copy of the POA?"

She quietly nodded 'yes.'

"I'm sure they saw the same thing I did. That's what this is all about. If Roger dies outside of Dallas they will come after you. They think they'll have a better chance of getting their money that way."

With the attorney's words the walls clapped shut with a bang – right on Patricia. She leaned forward and put her head between her knees while trying to take deep breaths. Stan got her some water and sat next to her. After a few minutes she sat back up and collected herself.

"What about his other debts? Am I liable for those, too?"

"It's a gray area. He accumulated those debts before you signed the POA, so you might be able to go to court. But, it would be expensive and might take months of fighting.

"Oh, my god! What am I going to do?"

"My first bit of advice to you is to find a way to get Roger back to Dallas. The insurance company said they would cover him if he is under his doctor's care. That means you need to do whatever it takes to get him back to his doctor. That will at least take care of the medical bills. Then we'll start working on the other bills. Take the hospital up on their offer and get up there as soon as you possibly can to bring him home before he dies."

"Why would the hospital offer to help me bring him home? They obviously want him to die outside of Texas."

"They're covering their butts. They don't think he'll make it back. And, by making the offer, they free themselves of any liability that they attempted to interfere. Based on what you said, I don't think it will be possible to get him home alive. Talk to his doctor in Dallas and make sure he knows everything that's going on."

She was still feeling weak and shaky, taking a few more moments to regain her strength.

"How will I ever tell John?"

§§§§§

John listened quietly while she explained the situation. It was a good thing since she was nearly in tears. When she was done she sat and waited for his recriminations. Instead, he simply looked at her and said, "Well, we better find a way to get Roger back to Dallas."

"You're not upset?"

"I'm certainly not happy about it, but it's my fault as much as it's yours. I encouraged you to do this and didn't think to have Stan look over the paperwork, either. We'll simply have to deal with it, that's all. What other choice do we have?"

She felt so thankful for him at that moment. He would have been fully justified if he had exploded, and she could see he was fighting hard to prevent exactly that. His support made all the difference.

"I can't believe Roger would do this to us."

"He probably didn't. Stan said it was a standard POA form. He probably got it off the Internet without ever checking on it."

John continued after a few moments, "Have you given any thought to how we can get him back down here?" Patricia was concerned with how he wouldn't look her in the eye. She knew he was on the edge.

"Yes. We have to drive him. He's too sick to go on a plane. Someone has to go up there, load him in a van and bring him back. I've already made the arrangements."

"What do you mean by 'someone'?"

This, she knew, was going to be the hard part.

"Ray Krieger."

He stared at her in shocked amazement before throwing his glass against the wall in anger. She flinched at his uncharacteristic display of anger. Of the two of them, he was always the calm one.

"That screw-up? What makes you think he can stay sober long enough to even get himself back, let alone someone near death?"

"Do you have a better suggestion? I can't go because I have to take care of all of the other estate needs. If I don't find a way to deal with his debts we'll be stuck with those, too. You can't go because you're the one holding the family together while I'm doing all of this. All of our friends have their own commitments and can't just get up and go. Same with his kids and everyone else he knows. And, it has to happen right away. Like tomorrow. He might not even last that long, so we can't wait. Who else can you think of?"

He leaned back in his chair, running his hands through his close-cropped hair and over his face.

"Have you even talked to him? What makes you think you can get him to do it?"

"Because I have to."

§§§§§

The small house Ray Krieger rented started its existence as a hunting cabin. As the population in the area grew, the hunting business went away and the cabin's owners turned to renting the cabin as a way to replace the lost income. Patricia had helped him find it and worked out a deal with the owners. The isolated location suited Ray well. He could drink and smoke marijuana and there wasn't anyone around to bother him.

The cabin wasn't bad, as cabins go. It had one bedroom and bath, a living area and a kitchen with a dining area. There was a large porch out front. In the old days, the hunters would sit out there and get drunk after a day in the field. Now, Ray liked to use it when he got stoned. That's where Patricia found him when she drove up. She had started the day saying goodbye to Roger at the hospital in Idaho Falls, unaware of the shocks coming her way. Now, the idea of sitting on the porch while watching the Texas sunset seemed like a good idea.

The gravel in the caliche-covered dirt road that served as a driveway crunched as she approached. Ray watched but didn't make any effort to acknowledge her.

Approaching thirty, he had a pleasant face framed by long, brown hair. The thing Patricia liked most about him was his neatness. He was always clean and his hair was always well groomed, even when he was stoned. He took care of his body, as well and his average-sized frame was slim but muscular. She was frustrated by the lack of ambition and willingness to spend his time stoned, but found he was someone she could trust. When he worked, he worked hard and didn't compromise. That was why she vouched for him at the nursery to do contract work. Basically lazy, she still felt he was someone she could depend on.

"Hello, Ray."

He tilted his head to one side and gave her a smile.

"Mrs. K! How are you? What brings you out this-a-way?"

She was holding a large envelope and placed it on the table next to Ray.

"I'm doing well, Ray. I have a job for you."

He gave the first indication he was paying any attention to her and turned to face her as he said, "Not today. I'm not much in the mood to do any more work today."

"It's not for today, but I need you to do it first thing tomorrow. It's really important and I'm counting on you."

"Whoa! You got the wrong guy if it's important. I don't do important."

He returned to staring out into space, watching the sunset sky, with a small smile. Patricia had been afraid it would be like this. Ray was reliable when he was sober. The problem was finding him sober. She knew when he got stoned he went into his own world and it could be hard to get him to come back out.

"Ray, I really need you to do this. I have something I want you to see."

She pulled out her phone and called up the video she took of Roger in the hospital, holding it up for Ray to see. He started to turn away, but when he saw the way Roger was straining and screaming, he couldn't stop looking. There is something about seeing the suffering of another human being that captures the attention of all of us. It is the human carnage of a traffic accident, the public display of a suicide, the victim of a murder. We are all the same when it comes to witnessing human suffering – we can't stop looking, even while we feel revulsion at the sight. Ray saw the suffering of Roger Tucci and felt his resistance starting to fade.

"Whoa! What are you showing me that for?"

"This is a friend of mine and he's the job I need you to do. He's in Idaho. He's in real trouble, and I need you to help him."

"I'm sorry he's suffering like that, but there's nothing I can do about it."

"No, there isn't. He's going to die and you can't stop it. But, if he dies in Idaho they will take everything I own. Just because I stepped up to help a friend."

48

Her words were finding a way through the dope-induced haze.

"I really don't know what I can do to help."

"I need you to go to Idaho and drive him back to Dallas. Ray, look at me. I really need you to go to Idaho for me. If no one brings him back, they will take everything I own. Do you understand that?"

"Why don't you do it yourself?"

"I can't. I have to take care of his estate. No one else can do that. If his business fails, they'll still take everything I own."

"What about your husband? Why not ask him?"

"He's taking care of the kids, the household, and doing his regular job, all at the same time. It would be disastrous if he dropped everything to make the trip. We've talked it over and looked at all of our options. There is no one else but you. Stay with me, Ray! I really need you to do this for me. I'm begging you. I really need you to do this. Please!"

There was no way he was going to go to Idaho to drive a dying man all the way to Dallas. It was totally crazy and it wasn't fair for her to ask him.

"Okay, I'll do it for you."

"Promise?"

"Yes, I promise."

Ray thought to himself, "Where in hell did that come from?"

She felt much better when she heard him say that. She had never known Ray to break a promise.

"Oh, thank you so much. Let me show you what you need to do."

She picked up the envelope and, while she was pulling out papers, without looking up, Patricia said, "Can I ask you something?" Without waiting for an answer, she asked, "Why do you get stoned so much?"

Ray shrugged one shoulder and said, "It relieves the boredom."

"Ray, I'm not talking about a little toking. I don't mind if you want to smoke some weed every now and then, but sometimes you're a real stoner. You can't spend your whole life getting stoned."

"Why not?" he asked. "I think it's working out just fine."

§§§§§

It was well before dawn when she picked him up the next morning. She had slept poorly and felt like it. Every time she had fallen asleep she had dreams of Roger tied to a bed while screaming and Ray laughing at her while saying he had changed his mind. It was a major relief when she arrived at the cabin to find Ray sober and ready to go. Her plan was to drive him to DFW airport and continue to Roger's office to figure out what was going on with his finances.

As they drove in the dark, she briefed him on the plan she had worked out.

"Your flight from DFW goes to Salt Lake City and you change planes. You have a one hour lay-over, so you shouldn't have any problems if the planes are on time. The flight from Salt Lake City to Idaho Falls is non-stop and you'll get there before one in the afternoon. Take a taxi to the truck rental place. I made the arrangements and they'll be expecting you. Then, go to the hospital to get Roger. I've cleared everything with them. The orderlies will strap the gurney into the van and load him for you while the doctors and nurses will give you the training you'll need. They'll also have all of the paperwork you'll need to sign. I made sure everything is ready. I put directions to everything in that envelope along with all of the forms I needed to sign. I also included the best route to take. The trip will take about 24 hours of driving. I don't want to put Roger through the strain of getting in and out of the van, so you'll have to sleep in the van when you make stops." She handed him another envelope. "This should be enough to cover your expenses. Keep all of your receipts. If you need to spend more money let me know and I'll reimburse you. I checked the weather up there. It's cold, but not too bad. You know, Idaho in February. What do you expect? There's a storm coming late tonight, but you should be able to stay ahead of it."

She hesitated before continuing.

"Ray, there's something you need to be aware of. Given the amount of time it's going to take you, you need to be prepared. Roger is going to need to go to the bathroom."

"Yeah. We all do it."

"Yes, but we don't all wear diapers."

50

It took a few seconds for that to sink in.

"Wait! You mean I'm going to have to change his diaper?"

"Yes. That's what I mean. I want you to be ready for it."

She thought he was about to open the car door and jump out while she was driving down the highway.

"Ray! I know it's something you would prefer not doing, but think of it from Roger's viewpoint. This is a proud man and now he's reduced to the point of having someone else changing his diapers for him. How do you think he feels about that? Just be ready. The hospital will give you some fresh diapers and wipes. When it happens, just take the dirty diaper off, clean him up and put a new diaper on. Please don't make him feel any worse than he already is. Can you do that?"

"You're lucky you didn't tell me this detail in the beginning."

"It wasn't luck."

They rode a while in silence before she continued.

"They'll give you morphine for the trip. Don't get caught with it, even with a doctor's script. They'll show you how to administer it and give you instructions about his IV. Also, they'll give you some food he can eat. It has to be soft and you'll have to feed him. He's aware when he's awake, but very limited. I gave you a toy clicker. Put it in his hand so he can call you when he needs something. He can talk a little, but not much."

Ray stared out the car window as he said, "He must have been a good friend for you to do all of this for him. This must all be hard on you."

"Yes, he was a very good friend and it is very hard on me. I'm going to miss him and I hate seeing him like this."

"Tell me about him. What was he like?"

For the rest of the trip to the airport she told him stories of Roger. She told him about how she met him, showing up topless at his house, and the way she and John had become good friends with him over the years and about how he was a brilliant businessman. She told him about how generous Roger had always been, about how he was always there to help someone out or to support a cause. She told him about his three children and his ex-wife. She also told him about his faults, about how he could be taken advantage of so easily and how he was a serial philanderer unable to keep away from women.

"He has this amazing ability to see people. What I mean is, he will actually look at someone and notice things. Combine that with his ability to read body language and sometimes it's like he's reading minds. It's pretty uncanny."

"And, I've never known anyone who can make decisions the way he can. He isn't always right, but he's right more often than anyone else I know. He says he looks at all the options, eliminates the ones he can't do and that usually leaves only a few choices. I've tried it and it works sometimes, but you have to be able to see all of the options to make it work. That's what he's good at. Seeing those options."

She continued telling him stories and by the time they reached the airport, Roger was no longer a guy screaming in pain while strapped to a hospital bed - he was a man, someone with a life and a history.

Ray stopped as he was getting out and hesitated before he said, seriously, "Don't worry, Patricia. I'll get him home. I promise." With that, he closed the car door and went into the terminal.

Interlude

"Good evening, gentlemen. I'm Sophie. I'll be serving you tonight. May I start you out with a drink while you look over the menu?"

"Thank you, Sophie. I'll have a whiskey on the rocks," said Roger, looking her in the eyes.

"I'll have the same," said Paul, without looking up.

The two men continued to talk until Sophie returned with their drinks.

"Do you need some more time to look over the menus or are you ready to order?"

Paul was busy looking over the menu and asked for some more time. When she turned to Roger, he said, "What do you recommend, Sophie? What's good today?"

"The *Lenguado al Limón al Horno* – pan-seared fresh lemon sole fillet – is excellent tonight. The chef tosses it in flour, salt and pepper before cooking it in olive oil and butter and topping it off with freshly squeezed lemon juice. The touch of lemon brings out the flavor in a very pleasant way and the sole is fresh and tender. If you pair it with the Santa Rita Reserva Chardonnay you won't be disappointed."

"That sounds excellent. Thank you, Sophie," he said. Seeing that Paul wasn't ready to order, he took the opportunity to flatter the young woman.

"May I say you are looking very lovely tonight? That shade of lipstick brings out the color of your skin very nicely. And, it goes well with your beautiful eyes."

Sophie was a little taken aback by his comments, but managed to keep her composure, even feeling flattered by the attention.

"Thank you, sir. That's very nice of you to say. Are you from here or are you in town for business?"

"My companion is from here, but I'm in town for a few days to take care of some business. I'm always looking for business opportunities. Maybe you know of something?"

He handed her his menu, allowing his hand to linger on hers for just a brief moment while looking her in the eyes and smiling. Surprising herself, she didn't pull away. She found herself very attracted to him and couldn't understand it. She was normally very resistant to men's advances, but it was as if this guy had cast a spell over her.

Paul handed his menu to her and said, "I'll have the spring chicken with fresh mushrooms. And, could I have a glass of that chardonnay?"

"Very well, sir. May I suggest pairing this dish with the Domados Cabernet Sauvignon from Argentina? It will sit on the palate very pleasantly."

"No, I think I'll stick with the chardonnay."

"Yes, sir. Your dinners will be out shortly." She returned Roger's smile before leaving.

They discussed their business venture over their dinners, Roger enjoying his meal more than Paul. He savored every bite while Paul simply ate. Sophie stopped by on occasion to check on them. Each time, Roger interrupted what he and Paul were discussing and smiled as he looked her in the eye and told her how excellent his dinner was, adding a seemingly random comment at the same time. She started making comments in return and smiled back before moving on.

Paul finally realized Roger was flirting with their waitress and said, "How do you do it, Roger? How do you get so many women to go to bed with you?"

"That's the thing, Paul. I never try to get a woman to go to bed with me. I convince them to try and get me to go to bed with them."

"I don't get the difference."

"For you, it's all about getting laid. You want to put a notch in your bedpost. It's never that way with me. I want them to put a notch in their bedposts. I want to make them feel beautiful and desired. I want them to look in a mirror and be happy with what they see. For you, it's all about you. For me, it's all about them. They can tell. Women are as beautiful as we men make them believe they are."

"Come on, Roger! You can't tell me you're some kind of special breed of male, that you're different than the rest of us. I bet you don't have a single female friend you haven't gone to bed with."

"Yes, I do. You're mixing up sex with making someone feel special. There are many ways to make a woman feel beautiful without taking her to bed."

"And, you say you can pick up any woman?"

"I have never claimed I could pick up a woman. What goes on between a woman and me is our business and I don't go around bragging."

"Okay, for the sake of argument, *could* you pick up any woman?"

"No, definitely not any woman. There are plenty of women who are happy with who they are and with their lives and don't need me, or anyone else, to tell them they're special. They already know it. Some aren't attracted to me. Then there are the ones that are attracted and like to flirt, but that's all. I'm okay with that. I'm not trying to set some kind of record. I just like pleasing women. I think a happy woman is the most wonderful thing in the world."

"I think you're full of it. I'll tell you what. I'll bet you dinner you can't pick up our waitress."

"Sophie. Her name is Sophie."

"Fine. Sophie."

"And, she's not a waitress, she's a chef."

"How could you possibly know that?"

"She's wearing a chef's smock, not the uniform the wait staff are wearing. When I asked her what she would recommend, she recommended something right away, told me how it was cooked and she was able to pronounce it correctly. On top of that, she knew what wine to pair it with. By the way, you should have accepted her recommendation on the wine, she knows what she's doing. She also checks on the waiters and waitresses and advises them. She's doing an internship here and hopes to open her own restaurant someday. You would know that if you had thought of her as something more than a fling in bed. Did you even notice the color of her hair?"

"Blond."

"Good guess, but wrong. She has auburn hair."

"The offer is still good. I'll give you until the end of dinner to get her to go out with you. You don't have to go to bed with her, just get her to go out."

At that moment, Sophie walked up and asked, "Is there anything else I can get for you gentlemen tonight?" She was looking right at Roger and put her hand on his arm when she said it.

He lightly put his hand on top of hers. "No, we're fine, thank you. That was an excellent meal, Sophie. Thank you for the recommendation. Could we have our check, please?"

She nodded and handed Roger the billfold with their check.

Roger said, "I think dinner is on me, tonight," as he inserted his credit card in the billfold and handed it back to her. She quickly returned with the credit card receipt for him to sign.

"Thank you gentlemen for coming in. I hope you have a pleasant evening."

Roger signed the receipt and returned it to the billfold. As the two men were leaving the restaurant, Roger placed his copy of the receipt into his pocket, along with the note that had come with it. "Call me, Sophie," it read, followed by a phone number.

Chapter Five

Ray checked his email while waiting in the terminal in Salt Lake City for his connecting flight and saw he had an email from Patricia.

"Just wanted to remind you of why you're doing this," the email read. There was an attachment that opened automatically when he downloaded it. It was Roger pulling at his restraints and screaming in pain. Ray quickly shut it down, but not before getting some looks from the people around him.

"It's a video of a guy dying from cancer," he explained to the man sitting next to him. "He's a friend of a good friend of mine. I'm going up to Idaho to bring him home for her."

"She must be a good friend. Are you sleeping with her?"

Ray was surprised by the question.

"No! Why would you ask a stranger a question like that?"

"I saw that video. That would have to be one damn good friend."

"Well, no, I'm not sleeping with her. And, yes, she's a good friend."

With that, he got up and changed seats.

§§§§§

Once in Idaho Falls, he took a taxi to the address Patricia had provided for the van rental. While he was filling out the paperwork, the clerk asked him if he wouldn't mind taking a smaller van at a lower rate. They had an unexpected demand for vans and needed every one they could get.

"Let me see it," he said.

The clerk took him out to see the van. When Ray climbed in the back and lay down his feet were sticking out the back door.

"No, this won't work. I need the larger one we reserved."

The clerk had watched this in silence, but finally had to ask, "What was that all about?"

Ray looked at him and finally confessed, "I need to take a dying man back to Dallas. He'll be in a gurney in the back. The van you offered wasn't long enough."

"He must be a good friend for you to do this."

"I've never met him. He's a friend of a friend. She's a good friend, though."

"Are you sleeping with her?"

"What are you talking about?"

"I'm sorry. I didn't mean to offend you. It's just that it would take a lot to get me to do something like that."

"No, I'm not sleeping with her. There are other reasons to be friends with a woman, you know."

"Yes, sir. I know. Again, I apologize for my comment."

Ray let it slide, but he had to wonder about the way people around him thought.

§§§§§

Patricia had advised him to call the hospital once he had the van so they would be ready when he arrived. He drove the van to the hospital receiving area and as he got out he was met by a team walking out the doors. One small group of orderlies had a legless gurney with them and went straight to the back door of the van. Before Ray could even talk to them they were inside strapping the gurney bed in place. A couple of men approached him.

"I'm Haywood Alban. I've been handling the patient's case. This is Dr. Eric Seabolt. He's the doctor in charge. Are you Ray Krieger?" Ray nodded. "Good. I was told you have some papers for me."

Ray handed him the signed papers Patricia had provided him. "I think this is what you want."

Alban and Seabolt took turns looking them over before the doctor nodded his approval.

"We'll need you to sign these documents acknowledging you took possession of the patient."

"Roger Tucci. And I want to see him first."

58

The doctor turned to the door and signaled to someone inside. A couple of orderlies appeared, rolling a gurney with a man strapped to it between them.

"This is the patient. Is that sufficient?"

Ray was beginning to feel angry and tried to stay calm as he said, "He has a name. His name is Roger Tucci."

Turning to Roger, he bent over and checked on him.

"Roger? Can you hear me?" Roger nodded his head slightly.

"Good. My name's Ray. I'm a friend of Patricia's. She asked me to take you home. Are you ready to go home Roger?"

Roger gave him another small nod and weak smile. Ray stood up straight and indicated the orderlies could move him into the van.

"These nurses will instruct you on how to care for the patient."

Once the orderlies were done putting Roger in the van, Ray, a nurse and the doctor all climbed into the van, making it crowded, but it was necessary to show Ray all he needed to know. The nurse quickly walked him through the handling of the IV and how to administer the morphine. He was provided a treatment schedule, along with some food and supplies. They were as warm as if they were buying produce at the grocery store.

When they were done with the training, Alban presented him with the papers to sign.

"Please sign at the marks acknowledging you received the patient and he was still alive."

"Roger Tucci. I told you, he has a name."

"Of course. If you'll simply sign these papers you can be on your way."

Ray returned the papers when he was done and Alban looked them over before saying he was satisfied. The three of them got out of the van and the administrator put several copies of the forms in an envelope, which he handed to Ray.

"Mr. Krieger, here are your copies of the forms."

Dr. Seabolt handed Ray a business card and told him, "Here's my card. Call if you have any questions."

Alban held out his hand and said, "Thank you for making this go smoothly. Good luck on your trip."

Instead of shaking his hand, Ray looked at the two of them and said, "You people are nothing but a bunch of fucking assholes. Worthless, fucking, assholes."

He then turned and headed for the van door. The doctor called after him, "Hey! You can't talk to us that way!"

Ray muttered to himself, "Just did!" as he got in the van and drove off, leaving the doctor and administrator standing in the cold air. He drove a short distance before pulling into the parking lot of a shopping center. Climbing into the back, he checked on Roger and made sure everything was secure. Ray was glad to see he was at least partly awake.

"Are you okay, Roger? Are you comfortable enough?"

Roger gently nodded his head.

"How about the pain?"

"It's fine," he whispered. "Why are you doing this?"

"Patricia Kennealy asked me to. She's a good friend. And no, before you ask, I'm not sleeping with her."

Roger smiled before telling him, "I know."

Ray produced the clicker Patricia had given him and put it in Roger's hand.

"Can you click that?"

His question was rewarded with a clicking sound.

"Good! We're going to drive down through Wyoming and will get on the Interstate there. It will take us around to Denver and down into New Mexico. We'll cut across to the Panhandle and then down to Dallas. It's going to be a long drive. If you need anything, just give a couple clicks and I'll hear it."

"Thank you for doing this."

He adjusted the blanket around Roger to make sure he was protected from the cold.

"Patricia told me about you. About how you've helped people and stood up for the right things over the years. And, she always was there to help me out. I'm glad to be able to help you and her."

Roger gave him a small smile and weakly nodded his head before falling asleep. Convinced everything was in good order, Ray climbed back into the driver's seat and began the long drive to Dallas.

Interlude

"I don't understand," she said. "Your advertisement said these dresses were on sale. Why do I have to pay full price?"

"If you read the ad, it says they are on sale only between 3 and 5 in the afternoon. It's nearly 5:30." The clerk pointed at the ad for emphasis. "It's marked very clearly right there. We do that to try and get people in during certain times of the day."

"I shop here frequently and you're going to tell me I have to pay almost twice as much because of 30 minutes?"

"I'm sorry ma'am, but that's what the ad says."

Kristen Sachs felt her anger rising and was about to explode when an amazingly good looking man interrupted.

"May I help? Maybe we can reach a compromise here and avoid any hurt feelings."

He looked from one woman to the next. His offer was so unexpected neither woman knew what to say and just looked at him.

"Good. Why don't we do this?" Turning to the shop clerk, he said, "Why don't you give her half of the discount. In return, this lovely woman will be glad to let it drop."

He turned to the clerk and looked her in the eyes as he placed his hand gently on top of hers and gave it a small squeeze.

"Your eyes are enchanting. It would be a shame to waste such beauty on a fight with a customer. Do you think you could do that for me?"

Without realizing it, the clerk found herself nodding her head in agreement.

"Wonderful!" He then turned to Kristen and lightly placed one hand on her shoulder as he looked her in the eyes and said, "So, lovely lady, would that work for you, too?"

He was nodding his head as he asked her and she found herself nodding also.

"There we go! See? Isn't that much better than arguing about it?"

Kristen paid for the dress, thanking the clerk as she turned to go. The man was just finishing his purchase at the next clerk and was about to leave at the same time.

"Thank you," she said as they walked out together. Extending her hand, she said, "I'm Kristen Sachs."

"Roger Tucci," he said as he took her hand in his. With dark hair and a classic figure, she was strikingly beautiful. "Are you doing anything right now, Kristen? Would you care to join me for a drink?"

Without knowing why, Kristen agreed.

Later, as she was getting dressed, she surveyed his apartment and appreciated the fine furniture and fixtures. He had told her he was a business owner, that he purchased small companies, fixed them up, and then sold them for a profit.

This, she thought, was a man that could keep a woman in style.

§§§§§

"I'm telling you, the guy is a woman whisperer."

The three ladies listening to her all laughed.

"A what?"

"A woman whisperer. You know, like that guy on TV with the dogs, except he does it to women."

Her friends – Janis, Roseanne and Corie – all laughed at this. The four women were enjoying their Friday evening happy hour as Kristen filled them in on her new male adventure.

"Really! You should see him. He can get just about any woman to do whatever he wants. They all get this dreamy look in their eyes and before you know it, they're doing anything he asks them to."

"And, what about you? Have you had a few dreamy eye moments?"

"I'll confess, I'm not completely immune."

"So, what's he like?" Janis asked.

"He's gorgeous. There's no denying that. And, he does real well. He could take good care of a woman."

"How old is he?"

"I think he's twenty-nine, so a few years older than I am."

63

"Did you have sex with him yet?" asked Roseanne.

Corie slapped at her arm while they all laughed.

"Of course. Men use sex as just another way to subjugate women. Why shouldn't we do the same to them?"

"Is that what you think? Men use sex to subjugate women? You don't enjoy it?"

"Are you crazy? Why would I enjoy a man putting his hands all over me? If it wasn't for the fact that we're in a world dominated by men and have to have sex with them, I think the population would dwindle to nothing."

"Well, I think he sounds wonderful," Janice said in an effort to change the subject. "When do we get to meet him?"

"Are you kidding? I'm not letting him anywhere near you floozies until I have him safely locked up. This one is a keeper."

"What are you planning to do?"

"I'm going to tell him all the things he wants to hear. I'll tell him what a great lover he is and how handsome he is. That part is true, so he'll believe everything else I tell him as a result. I'll be at his side in all of his social circles. I'll laugh when his friends make dumb jokes. In short, I'll be the perfect trophy girlfriend. Then, I'll be the perfect trophy wife. Roger won't know what hit him."

They all laughed, but her friends all understood. Kristen loved the good life and Roger was going to be her meal ticket.

§§§§§

Roger was no fool when it came to Kristen. He understood what was going on. She was a gold-digger. He got it. He also understood she was enchanting and made him feel good when they were together. It made it easy to introduce her to his friends and take her to business parties.

Roger's most recent venture was an engine parts supplier that was failing under the weight of declining business and rising expenses. Roger thought he could turn the business around by focusing on different engines. Jet skis and all-terrain vehicles were becoming the rage. As the number of these vehicles in the public increased, the number of service shops would also. The business already had the facilities and supply network to provide the tools and parts that would be needed. It would be a huge success. The only thing missing was the business itself. The current owner, Leslie Greene, refused to sell to Roger. He had built it from scratch and thought it was worth more than Roger could afford to pay. Greene was willing to watch the business fail rather than sell it for what Roger offered. Greene was wealthy and could afford it.

Roger used his skills to the best of his abilities, but he couldn't close the deal. Tonight, he was giving it one last try.

"I understand what you're saying, Leslie. You have an estimate of how much the business is worth, but I've shown you all of my estimates. Surely, you can see I'm offering as much as I can. If I were to pay any more, the business wouldn't be able to support itself."

"That's fine, Roger. I would love to close a deal with you, but you don't sell a Porsche at Chevy prices. If you want to do business, come up with the money. No hard feelings, Roger. You're a good guy. I just won't sell at the price you're offering."

Roger shrugged his shoulders in resignation.

"Well, Leslie, I'm sorry we couldn't do business, but I don't have any hard feelings either. Business is business and you've been straight with me the whole time."

The two men shook hands and parted. Roger found Kristen and told her the news.

"What are you going to do now?" she asked.

"There's always a deal to be made. I'll just move on from this one and find something else."

Kristen ran her finger along the edge of her wine glass while she thought.

"Give me a few minutes," she said before slipping away.

Greene was talking to a group of friends and she asked if she could join them. Greene recognized the tall brunette right away. She had the kind of figure a room full of men would immediately notice. And most of the women, too.

"You came with Roger. Let me guess, he sent you over to give me one last sales pitch."

"Roger doesn't even know I'm talking to you. This was all my idea."

"Well, you're wasting your time, sweetie. I already told Roger I won't sell at his price. I value the company more than that."

"And, I don't blame you Mr. Greene. You put a lot of hard work into building that business. You paid for it. Not just with the money you invested, but with the time and effort you put into it – the sweat equity. Not to mention the time away from your family. I guess you could even consider the business to be like one of your children."

"Sister, you can say that again. When I think of all of the things I missed because I had to be at the shop, I just cringe. Birthdays, little league, family vacation – you name it, I missed it."

"I understand. And now, you want your child to be treated right. You want respect for what you built."

"I guess you could put it that way. Yeah, respect."

"I can completely understand how you would rather close it down than sell for less than what you think it's worth. Give it a proper funeral, so to speak."

"Now, that isn't what I was saying."

"Well, you did say you would rather see it go out of business, didn't you? I think that would be the right thing to do. I don't think Roger would treat it the same way you have. To him, it's a business. He wants to turn it around and sell it someday. He doesn't look at the way you do. It isn't one of his children. Know what I mean? You should put it out its misery. It would be a mercy killing."

Two days later, Greene called Roger and accepted the offer.

"By the way, that's quite a girl you have there, Roger."

§§§§§

The wedding was beautiful. Kristen had insisted on spending a great deal of Roger's money and the result was memorable. Her three friends, all bridesmaids, gathered together after the ceremony.

Roseanne told her two friends, "You know what she said to me this morning? She said they had sex last night and she bragged about how it was the last time she was ever giving someone a blow job."

"It's kind of funny, when you think about it," commented Janice. "The only woman that is immune to his talents is the one that should be enjoying them the most."

"I give them six months." This from a skeptical Corie.

Janice disagreed. "No, I think they'll last longer than that. I say five years."

Roseanne shook her head. "You're both wrong. Kristen won't let her meal ticket get away that easily. She trapped him into the marriage; she'll trap him into staying."

"How?"

"Children. Every time she thinks she's losing control of him, she'll have another baby. Roger is the kind of guy who won't leave his kids. He'll stay around for as long as he needs to in order to take care of them. If she isn't the perfect mother, he'll make up for it by hanging around to be the perfect dad. I give them 25 years, at the minimum."

Janice shook her head, "I've never seen a woman so alone. That is going to be one miserable marriage."

"Only for one of them. But, she would be miserable no matter who she married. The other one will always find a way to have fun. And I think I'll be sure to be around to help him."

"Why, Roseanne! You sound like you've been sampling the honey," said Corie with a fake look of surprise.

"And you two haven't?"

The other women both had a conspiratorial smile as they shrugged their shoulders and laughed.

"Well, it looks like we're all thinking the same thing."

Kristen saw her friends talking together and wondered what they were laughing about. She was sure it was some silly talk about sex. She couldn't understand why those three thought sex was so interesting. To her, it was a tool to control men, something that happened on occasion, but nothing to get worked up about.

She recalled an old joke someone told her years ago. Scientists had found a food that killed a woman's sex drive - wedding cake. She didn't get it when she first heard it, but she did now. She sighed contentedly as she thought of how her days of having to seduce men were over.

Chapter Six

The drive along the Palisades Reservoir in Idaho had been beautiful, but slow, and he knew he was behind schedule. The highway was two lanes with a lot curves due to the terrain, preventing him from speeding up. Still, the map said this was the fastest route. He was glad to see the sign welcoming him to Wyoming. Highway 26 got straighter in this area and he was making better time. Ray was admiring the frozen, but still spectacular vista he was driving through when the radio DJ announced the weather report.

"The National Weather Service has updated their forecast for the incoming winter storm. The weather system that wasn't supposed to reach us until late tonight will instead be moving into the listening area late this afternoon or early evening. Temperatures are expected to plunge into the minus-double digits with widespread heavy snow. Travelers are advised to use caution."

Ray turned off the radio in frustration. He had been hoping to stay ahead of the worst of the storm.

Great! What are we going to do now? he wondered to himself before he heard the clicking from behind him. Turning to glance behind him he said, "Roger. What's up, buddy?" Then, he smelled it and knew what the problem was.

"Oh. I get it. Let me find a place to pull over."

A wide spot on the shoulder provided enough room he felt safe stopping. The late afternoon light was fading quickly and it was getting gloomy outside. *This is it,* he thought. He braced himself, and, leaving the engine running for the heater, he climbed in the back to check on Roger.

"I'm sorry," the sick man mumbled.

"Don't sweat it, man. I'm all ready to take care of you. Let me get a clean diaper and we'll get you all fixed up."

Even with the heater on maximum, it was still chilly in the back and he didn't want to expose Roger to the air any more than necessary. He lifted the blanket up only as far as necessary, keeping Roger's upper body covered. Working quickly, he got the soiled diaper off and was busy cleaning his patient when the bright light from a flashlight played over the scene.

69

"Oh, man. What's this all about?"

He quickly climbed back into the front of the van, just to find a highway patrol officer standing at the window.

"Sir, please come out of the vehicle. Keep your hands where we can see them."

Ray looked at Roger, laying on his side with his lower body exposed to view.

"Oh, man. This is not going to go well."

"Sir! I said to come out of the vehicle. I'm not going to ask again."

Ray put his hands up where they could be seen before answering, "Okay! I'm coming out."

He made his way to the rear door, pulling the blanket down to cover Roger on the way. He stepped out into the cold mid-afternoon sunlight and faced the officer.

"Hello, officer. We were just taking care of an emergency. That's all."

"I could see what you were doing. Get over there. We'll be right with you."

At that point Ray realized a second officer had come from the front of the van where he must have been covering him from the other side.

"Everything is okay, officer. Let me explain."

"I said to get over there. We'll be right with you."

With that, the officer opened the door and looked in.

"Sir? Are you alright?" he asked Roger.

When he didn't get a response he climbed in and checked on Roger, who was barely awake. The officer checked on the IV and pulled Roger's eyelid back to check his pupils then checked his pulse. Finally, he climbed back out of the van and turned to Ray.

"What the hell is going on here?"

"Please, could you close the van doors? He's very sick. You're letting the heat out." Ray was rubbing his arms and jumping up and down in an attempt to keep warm himself. Grudgingly, one of the officers did as he asked.

"I looked in and saw you molesting this man. Is that right?"

"What? No! That isn't what was going on at all. He had a dirty diaper and I was changing it for him."

"A dirty diaper."

"Yeah. It's still in there. Take a look for yourself. Listen, I'm freezing. Can I please get my coat? It's on the passenger seat."

The second officer walked around and returned after a few seconds holding Ray's coat.

"This isn't going to keep you very warm," he said as checked the pockets before handing it to Ray.

"Yeah, well I didn't expect to be here for long. I'm trying to drive straight through to Texas."

"Texas. With a man strapped to a gurney and wearing diapers."

The officers could clearly see how nervous Ray was.

"Yes, sir. He has cancer real bad and I need to get him to his doctor in Dallas."

"Do you have a license and registration?"

Ray was glad to be finally asked something more normal and got his wallet out to turn over his driver's license.

"This is a rental van. The rental agreement is in the glove compartment."

The second officer took the driver's license to the patrol car while the first one continued questioning Ray.

"Suppose you tell me what's going on?"

"The man in there, Roger Tucci, has terminal cancer. He was in Idaho Falls when he had a stroke. The insurance company insisted he be moved back to Texas, so I flew up here to do that. He's not strapped in to the gurney. He has a safety belt on, but his arms are free. He's too weak to get out of bed so he's wearing an adult diaper. When you first saw me I was changing his diaper. That's all it was."

"Why is he so unresponsive?"

"He's on painkillers."

"Yeah, I saw the bottles of morphine."

"And, I have a doctor's script for that."

"How much of it have you been sampling?"

"I don't do morphine. A little pot sometimes, but nothing serious."

"You have any pot with you now?"

"No, sir. You can search the van, if you want. I'm clean."

Ray knew this was not going well, and he was really afraid of the next question.

"But, you brought that morphine over from Idaho Falls. That means you took it across the state line."

First a molester and now a drug smuggler. He sure hoped Patricia appreciated what he was doing for her.

The officer glared at him before saying, "Wait here." He then went back to the patrol car and Ray could see the two of them talking, occasionally looking up at him. Ray was about ready for them to arrest him if they would just take him somewhere warm, when the two officers got out of the patrol car and approached him.

"I'm not sure what's going on here, Mr. Krieger, but we decided to take you in until we can get it cleared up."

"Listen, officer. Can I show you something?"

The two patrolmen were suspicious as Ray got his phone out and called up a video.

"Take a look at this," he said as he held the phone up for them to see. The image of Roger in the hospital bed, screaming in agony, captivated the two officers and they watched in silence.

"That's Roger before they got his medication right. If you take him away you're either going to need to administer his painkiller yourself or this is what you'll be dealing with in a couple of hours."

The officers looked at each other, still silent.

Ray reached into his coat pocket and found the card they had given him at the hospital. "Here's the doctor's number. Call him and he'll verify everything I've been telling you." He suddenly wished he hadn't called the doctor a worthless fucking asshole.

The first officer took the card and looked at it before handing it back to Ray.

"I'll tell you what, Mr. Krieger. Against my better judgment, we're going to let you go. I just feel there's something you're not telling us, but I think there's enough truth we don't want to hold you. Here's your license. You can go."

The feeling of relief overwhelmed Ray and he almost danced as he made his way back to the van.

"Thank you, officer. I hope you guys have a great day!"

Ray got in the van and drove off before they had a chance to change their minds, being careful to signal he was getting back on the highway.

As the officers got back in the patrol car the second one said, "Have you ever seen anything like that before?"

"Are you kidding? I've never even heard of anything like that."

The junior officer asked, "How do you want to write this up?"

"Write up what?" was the only response.

The other officer merely nodded in agreement and didn't say anything more.

§§§§§

After putting a few miles behind him, he again looked for a place to pull over so he could finish what he had started with Roger. After getting him dressed and properly tucking the blanket around him, he offered Roger something to eat.

"I have some apple sauce here. Do you want some? Are you hungry?"

Roger barely shook his head and Ray put the container down.

"Roger, we're in trouble. There's a bad winter storm coming. I'm afraid they're going to close the roads and we won't be able to get through. I don't know what to do."

Roger said something but it was so faint Ray barely heard it.

"What can't I do? Is that what you said?"

Roger gave a slight nod.

"Well, the trip wasn't supposed to take more than a day. Patricia only gave me enough money for gas and food. I don't have enough for a room too, so we can't check into a motel. The van isn't warm, so we can't stay in the van if it gets too cold. If they close the roads we won't be able to drive through. I'm afraid to go to a shelter with you and the morphine. It was really close with the highway patrol. I don't want to risk that again."

"Sounds like you don't have many options. Makes the decision making easy," Roger whispered.

"I don't get it."

73

Roger took so long to answer Ray was afraid he had fallen asleep. "What do you have left?" he finally said.

Ray shook his head and slapped his hands on his thighs in frustration.

"I don't know. We have to get off the road. What can I do to pay for a room? Maybe I could barter something?" He looked around the van to see what he had available to trade and didn't find anything. "Maybe I could work for lodging. How about that? Do you think I can do that?"

Roger smiled and gave a small nod. "See? Once you narrowed it down it was pretty easy. Just get rid of the things you can't do and look at the things you can."

Ray checked the IV and saw Roger had drifted back to sleep. Once he was sure his patient was safe and comfortable, he climbed back in the driver's seat and got back on the road.

"Right. Work for lodging. Now, I just need to find some lodging."

§§§§§

U.S. Highway 26 wound north into the mountains and the Gros Ventre Wilderness area until Ray came to the turnoff for Highway 191. He pulled over and considered his options. It was already dark, but still early and he wanted to drive as far as he could. Straight ahead was the town of Hoback. The idea of possibly finding a place to ride out the storm sounded appealing, but it was to the north and that wasn't the direction he needed to go. To his right was Highway 191. It led to the south and Rock Springs at the Interstate, but that was a good three hours away. Ray knew having Roger in the back of the van wasn't supposed to be a long-term thing; he needed to be in a hospital. He thought it was more likely the Interstate would be cleared first. He needed to get to Rock Springs in order to get on that highway – down Highway 191.

Ray looked over his shoulder and saw Roger was still asleep. "No guts, no glory," he mumbled to himself. With that he turned to the right and headed for Rock Springs, hoping he would be able to stay ahead of the storm, or at least the worst of it.

§§§§§

The road was in good condition and it took only an hour to reach Pinedale. It was a town of about 2000, but compared to the wilderness he had been driving in it looked like downtown Manhattan. He pulled into a gas station and checked on Roger, finding him still sleeping deeply. He went into the convenience store to use the rest room, get something to eat and pay cash for the gas before heading out to fill the van.

The air was clear and crisp and the scenery he had seen during the day was soulfully beautiful.

"Yeah, I can see why someone would want to live here," he thought as he pumped the gas.

When he was done he got back into the van and thought he should probably give Roger another morphine shot. Climbing in the cramped back he said, "Roger? Are you awake? How're you feeling? I asked inside and they said we should be able to make Rock Springs before the storm gets here."

Ray crouched down next to him and checked to see how he was doing. After a few seconds he pulled the blanket back enough to reach the inside of Roger's wrist. After several tries he leaned back against the side of the van and quietly said, "Rest in peace, buddy."

Interlude

The nurse looked up as Roger entered the room.

"Could you excuse us, please?"

She looked skeptical, but turned to the woman in the bed.

"It's okay. We would like to be alone."

The nurse examined the monitors and wasn't happy with what she saw.

"Your vital signs are not very strong. I really should stay here."

"Your sitting here won't make my vital signs any better."

Reluctantly, the nurse left. Once alone, Roger pulled a chair up next to her and took her hand as he sat.

"I didn't want you to know. I didn't want anyone to know, but I especially didn't want you to know."

"I've known for a while but stayed away. I knew you didn't want sympathy."

"You have always been so perceptive. You were my best student."

"You had a way of keeping my attention."

She laughed at his comment. Quietly, they spoke of their time together over the years. They talked about the first time she seduced him, over 30 years earlier. He was just a teenager and she had asked him to help her carry the groceries in. Once in the house he was powerless to resist her advances.

They laughed at the memory. Finally, they paused and were silent for a few seconds.

"You're beautiful," he told her, breaking the silence.

"I'm an old woman," she objected.

"You're still very beautiful. One of the most beautiful women I've ever seen."

"When other men say something like that, it sounds like lip service. When you say it, it sounds real."

"What can I say? You were more than my teacher, you were my muse."

"Oh, Roger. We had us a good time, didn't we?"

"We sure did," he said as he gently squeezed her hand.

"You've done well. I'm very proud of you."

Her words meant as much to him as if they had come from his parents.

She took a deep breath before saying, "Thank you for coming. Now, I need you to do something special for me. I need you to leave and not look back. Can you do that, please? Don't say anything more."

He bent over and kissed her before rising and silently left the room.

When he was gone it occurred to her there was something wrong with the lights. She tried to raise herself to check on them, but didn't have the strength. That's when she realized she couldn't feel her legs anymore. No, there was nothing wrong with the lights. She calmly relaxed and thought about all of the years of good times. She was still smiling when they found her.

Chapter Seven

Ray felt a great deal of relief as he reached the outskirts of Rock Springs two hours later. Highway 191 was now five lanes wide and there was little traffic, but the heavy, blowing snow was making driving difficult. At first there had been tracks from other vehicles but now the only tracks he could see were nearly filled with snow. No one else had been driving down this road for a considerable amount of time. The locals all knew to get off the street.

Even with the heater blowing on high it was getting cold inside the vehicle. He didn't want to get stranded out in the wide-open spaces he had been driving in since leaving Idaho Falls. He could imagine himself ending up in some quirky newspaper article, "Man freezes to death in van while transporting dead body."

His focus was on the road while also searching through the blowing snow to find a motel, when he spotted the White Mountain Inn and, with a sigh of relief, pulled into the parking lot, noticing there were only a few cars there.

"This one's as good as any, I guess."

The snow was so heavy he couldn't see the stripes for the parking spots. He didn't want to take the chance someone might look in the back of the van and parked a short distance from the office, backing into the space with the rear end facing a fence to make it even more unlikely someone would look in.

Getting out of the van, he thought it was so cold the air even smelled cold. Rushing to get inside, he entered the empty office and rang the bell on the counter, only to have a beautiful woman come in from the back. Not only did the brunette have a perfect shape and a face to die for, but Ray couldn't help but notice she had the most incredible cleavage he had ever seen.

As she approached the counter she asked, "Can I help you?"

Ray quickly glanced at her amazing cleavage but was determined to not stare at her assets. He was sure that is what all the guys did and he was going to be different. He needed to make a deal with her and he didn't want to spoil his chances by burying his eyeballs between her breasts, no matter how perfect they were.

79

Focusing on her eyes, he said, "Hello, ma'am. I hope you can help me out. I'm trying to drive to Texas, but the snow is blocking the highway. They closed the Interstate going east from here and I need to find a room until it's clear."

"Well, I have plenty of rooms right now." She slid the registration card his way and said, "Fill out the registration here, if you don't mind."

"There's a problem. See, I wasn't planning on staying anywhere and I don't have enough money. I only have money for gas and meals."

"So, you're looking for a handout?"

"No, ma'am. I'm just wondering if maybe I could work for my room. I'm a handyman back home and I would be glad to work for my rent, if that's okay with you."

Ray's eyeballs had a mind of their own and kept trying to look down at her magnificent cleavage, but he was determined and forced them to focus on the woman's eyes. She could see he was fighting the urge to look down her blouse. It had been a slow day and, with the storm coming in, promised to stay that way. She decided to have a little fun at his expense and leaned forward over the counter to give him a good view while she thought about his offer.

"How do I know I can trust you? What's to keep you from taking advantage of me? Or, starting a job and leaving it unfinished? Or, just doing a crappy job?"

Ray could see her cleavage out the edge of his vision and felt the sweat forming on his forehead and upper lip.

"I can leave the keys to my van with you. I won't be going anywhere until you give them back. Will that work?"

"You're working real hard not to look, aren't you" she asked with a slow, husky voice and a smile.

He didn't even try to pretend he didn't know what she was talking about. "Looking at your beautiful eyes makes it easier."

"Smooth," she said with a laugh. "You're in luck stranger. I have some things I want done while it's slow. Fill out the registration card." She turned and thought a few seconds before selecting a key. Handing it to Ray, she said, "Room 1 is next to the office. Once you get settled in come on back with the key to the van. I'll put together a list of things to do."

Ray paused as he left the office and rubbed the side of his head.

"Holy shit! I think I pulled a muscle in my eyeballs. If cleavage was a superpower that woman would rule the world."

He went to the van to get his overnight bag. He took a look at Roger and said to the dead body, "You'll be okay. The cold won't hurt you none. This storm should last only a day or two and then we'll be on our way again."

He locked the vehicle and put his bag in the room before returning to the office. She was reading the registration card when he came back in. Handing her the car keys he said, "As promised."

She held out her hand and he shook it.

"Well, Ray Krieger, from Cisco, Texas. I'm Lynn Manzarak. Welcome to Rock Springs, Wyoming."

§§§§§

Even though it was already well into the evening, Ray went right to work on the list of chores Lynn gave him. The list ranged from minor maintenance chores to repairs for damage from unruly customers all the way to a couple of major jobs he doubted he would be able to tackle in just a couple of days.

He took out his phone and gave it some thought. He knew he needed to call Patricia, but he couldn't bring himself to do it. The drive from Pinedale had given him time to think about what he was going to do and he didn't want to involve Patricia. He had made a promise and there was only one way to keep it. It would be better if she didn't know anything about it, he thought, although he knew he would have to pay a price when he finally saw her again.

He was finishing up in one of the rooms and was thinking about seeing if he could find something to eat when Lynn showed up with a tray of food. The room had the standard furniture consisting of a couple of arm chairs and a small table.

"I thought you might be getting hungry," she said as she put the meal on the table.

"Thank you, I was. I wasn't expecting you to feed me, though."

"You'd have a hard time finding a place to eat tonight. The roads are closed. You'd have to get chips and soda out of the machine. Besides, I was impressed with how you went right to work."

"It was quite a list of chores you gave me. It's going to take some time to get through it all."

"I didn't mean for you to do everything. That's my to-do list. Anything you can knock off it will help."

They chatted while eating the meal together, both glad to have the company during a winter storm. Lynn was surprised to find herself attracted to Ray. She could see there was a lot to like, but she reminded herself he was only passing through. Don't get attached, she told herself.

"Are you from Rock Springs?" he asked between bites.

"No, I grew up in Cheyenne."

"How did you end up owning a motel out here?"

"My father is pretty well off and when I decided I wanted to major in hospitality management, he could afford to send me to the University of Denver. Their Fritz Knoebel School of Hospitality Management is one of the top schools in the country for the major. After I graduated I got a job working out east. I was very good at it and made a lot of money, but wasn't very happy.

"When I came home for a vacation, some friends were heading out for the Wyoming Chocolate Festival here and brought me along. This place always has something going on. Well, I fell in love with the town. It was everything I missed about living in Wyoming. The clear air, the mountains, the big views, the cowboy lifestyle. I don't think anyone raised in the northeast would understand it, but I really love this life.

"I decided right then and there this is where I wanted to live. I didn't exactly ditch my friends, but I went off on my own and starting looking for a place to buy. The problem was there wasn't anything for sale. Most of the places around here are either B&Bs people run out of their homes or chain motels like Best Western and Holiday Inn Express. I checked into everything I could find and talked with agents and came up with nothing. I was really bummed out about it.

"On our last morning here, we were having breakfast at a diner and I was telling my friends about my big, fat failure when this old gentleman came over. 'Excuse me,' he said. 'I didn't mean to listen in, but I couldn't help over hearing your conversation. If you're serious about finding a motel to buy, I can help you out.' It turned out he owned the White Mountain Inn and wanted to retire. He had been thinking about it for a long time without making up his mind. That's why none of the agents knew it might be for sale. Listening to me talk convinced him to go through with it. We reached an agreement that morning. When I flew back to New York I gave them my two-week notice and packed my things."

"What a story. That takes guts. How long have you been here?"

"This makes my fourth year. I haven't regretted it a single day."

"I guess this is the slow time of year. There aren't many cars in the parking lot."

"I get a few people passing through, but the ministers chase the hookers out of town for Lent, so it's pretty slow for a Friday night."

Ray shook his head before asking, "Did you just say the ministers chase the hookers out of town for Lent?"

"Well, 'chase' is a little strong. They talk to them and ask them to take a vacation. That way the guys can all say they're giving up hookers for Lent and they can still drink. It keeps the bars open. And, believe me, you don't want to close the bars up here in the middle of winter. It's about the only thing keeping people sane sometimes."

"So, I guess these girls provide you with a lot of business?"

"Oh, yeah. I have an arrangement with them. They charge their customers full fare for the room and I give them a little kickback."

"And that doesn't bother you?"

She shook her head as she said, "No, it's okay. I still make a profit."

Ray gave a low laugh, "No, I meant, doesn't it bother you to have the hookers bringing their business here?"

"Why would it bother me? They bring in a lot of money for me. What someone wants to do in private is none of my business. But, renting rooms in a motel is."

She had been looking over his work while they ate and had been impressed.

"That's good work."

"You do your own maintenance work?"

"As much as I can to keep costs down. I'm learning a lot, but I still have to contract out most of it. Mostly, I've learned to tell the difference between a good job and someone trying to rip me off."

"I understand. I don't like doing a half-assed job. If nothing else, it's good for business. I get a lot of repeat customers. Besides, I just like doing a good job."

She nodded in understanding, "How did you learn about fixing things up?"

He gave a lopsided shrug as he answered, "Trial and error. A lot of error, mostly. I did all of the house repairs as I was growing up."

"Where was your father?" she asked.

"He split when I was little. He's never been around since then. I don't even remember him."

"I'm sorry. I didn't think before asking. It's none of my business."

"No, it's okay. I don't mind. I didn't know anything else so it isn't a big deal for me. Neither of them wanted me and my mother got stuck. That was her term. 'Got stuck.' It wasn't bad. I mean, she cared for me alright. She kept me fed and bought me clothes and took me to the doctor when I was sick. But, she wasn't very loving."

"It doesn't bother you?"

"Like I said, I didn't know anything else. To me, that was the way life was supposed to be. My mother was pretty bad about keeping the house, so I learned how to do everything. I kept it clean and did the laundry, and I even became a pretty fair cook. Better than my mother, at least. She would put up with things being broken rather than pay a repair man. I got tired of it and did all of the repairs around the house. I really screwed things up at first, but I learned over time."

"Wasn't there anyone else around? Grandparents or aunts and uncles?"

"No. I don't know if my mother even had a family. The closest thing I had to a father figure was the old man across the street, Mr. Hardt, but it wasn't a movie kind of thing. He would yell and throw stuff at me if I came too close to his property. Everyone else just ignored me."

"Where's your mother now?"

"Beats me. After I finished high school, I took off for a while. I went back after a couple years and she had moved out. No one knew her forwarding address. I think of her, sometimes. But, there was no love lost between us. She didn't want me and I never learned to want her. So, I've been on the road ever since, doing work when I needed the cash. I'm pretty good at handyman stuff now and can find regular work, when I want. Mostly, I sit around and get stoned. It's a way to pass the time."

"Pass it until what?" she asked.

"What do you mean?"

"When people say they're passing the time, they normally mean they're waiting for something. What are you waiting for?"

He looked a little thoughtful before answering, "I really don't know. I've never thought about it. I guess until the next time I have to work to get some money. And, speaking of getting back to work, I won't finish this room if I don't get busy. Thank you for the dinner."

"You're welcome. Come by the office in the morning for some breakfast."

With that, she picked up the tray with the dishes and let herself out, pausing outside the door to briefly look back. She briefly let the thought cross her mind that it might be possible she could convince him he didn't need to wait any longer. But, then she shook her head and chased the thought away. *He's only passing through*, she reminded herself.

§§§§§

The storm was still raging in the morning with no hint it would be letting up anytime soon. Ray resigned himself to the idea he was going to be here for at least another day. He looked at the snow piled up in the parking lot as he made his way to the office. Someone would need to clear it if anyone was to get in or out. Fortunately, he thought, the snow was piled on the van, covering the windows and preventing anyone from accidentally looking in.

The warmth of the office was welcome after even the short walk from his room. His Texas-level coat was no match for the brutal cold of a Wyoming winter. He quickly closed the office door to shut off the flow of cold air following him in. Leaning against it, he became aware of the aroma of breakfast cooking. His stomach reacted to the smell and he immediately felt his appetite increase.

"Hello! Anyone home?" he called out.

"Come on back. Breakfast is about ready."

He walked around the front counter and through the door to find a surprisingly attractive apartment suite. The décor was very fashionable and clearly had a woman's touch. There wasn't a mounted animal head in the whole room. It looked like a modern apartment, not a frontier cabin, which is what he might have expected. The furniture was elegant and modern. To the left side was a living room while the other side was set up as a dining room. The table had already been set and Lynn came out of a door carrying plates of food. Ray could see the kitchen behind her. There was another door he supposed led to the bedroom.

"This is nice."

"Thanks. I had to fix it up when I bought the place. I don't think the previous owner had remodeled the whole time he lived here. He was a sweet, old man, but not much of a housekeeper. Have a seat. How do you like your coffee?"

"Black's good."

She handed him a mug and took a seat across from him.

"Thank you for the breakfast. This smells great."

"My pleasure. I don't get much company."

Ray noticed there wasn't anyone else there and caught her remark about a lack of company. Was she hinting, or was she merely being open and friendly?

"I was looking at the parking lot on my way over. The snow is really piling up. Do you have anyone to remove the snow?"

"I have a little Bobcat I use. I wouldn't want to clear roads with it, but it's fine for the size of the parking lot. I already spoke to all of my customers and they plan on staying here until the storm breaks, so there's no rush to clear the snow, but I'll have to get to it before it gets too deep. We normally get about 34 inches of snow a year. We might get close to that much in this one storm."

Once again, Ray noticed the lack of mention of any man.

"I'd offer, but I don't have very much experience with a Bobcat. I'm afraid I might tear up your parking lot."

"That's okay. If you can do the other things I can clear the snow. I won't be busy in the office today. The highways in and out of town are all closed for miles and they say the storm will last until sometime this afternoon."

Ray thought of Roger in the back of the van and how Patricia was waiting for them. Once again, he debated with himself if he should give her a call to tell her the news. On one hand, she would want to know. But, on the other hand, by not knowing she was innocent of anything he might do.

"What's the matter?"

Ray came out his thoughts and returned his attention to her.

"Oh, nothing. I was just thinking about my trip back. You know, thinking of what kind of changes I'll have to make because of the storm."

"I've been meaning to ask, just what are you doing up here?"

"A friend asked me to get some personal items from Idaho Falls and take them back to Dallas. She couldn't get time off to do it herself and I needed the work. I thought I'd be able to stay ahead of the storm and drive straight through. I wasn't planning on stopping anywhere."

Lynn nodded as she sipped her coffee, but thought there was something a little strained in his response.

§§§§§

Lynn used the Bobcat to clear the snow from the parking lot while Ray worked in the rooms. She eyed the trees as she worked and noted the snow building up in the branches. Trees could collect more snow than they could support, causing their branches to break. The falling branches were a hazard and could crush anything under them or bring down power lines. Besides, trees were few and far between in Rock Springs and Lynn valued hers.

Regular storms would keep the trees from getting too much new growth and kept the risk somewhat limited. But, it had been some years since they had seen a snow storm this severe and the trees had lots of long branches. Lynn walked around the property, inspecting any potential trouble spots, using a long pole to knock accumulation down where she could. Her reach was limited and her efforts still left a lot of snow covered branches. If it was just a case of a falling branch she didn't worry about it. But, if there were any places where it would cause some damage, then she would need to get Ray's help to take care of it. She noticed how she already thought of him as someone she could depend on.

The parking lot was the last area she checked. There were a couple of potentially bad places where she could just block the parking spaces and let the branches fall without hitting anything. But, she noticed Ray's van was parked right under a big tree loaded with snow. That, she knew, wasn't safe. Not wanting to interrupt his work, she went to the office and got his keys.

Since he had backed up into the parking space, the van was facing forward, making it easy to drive over the snow. She cleared enough of the windshield to see and was able to charge straight forward, parking it in a spot in front of the rooms. Locking the van door, she returned the keys to the office. The idea of doing something nice for Ray gave her an unexpected warm glow.

Once back in the office, she put together a couple of lunches and filled a thermos with hot coffee. Putting everything in a box, she carried it all down to the room where Ray was working, giving the door a quick knock before opening it. Ray was on his knees, plastering a hole in the wall where a drunken guest had kicked it in. Lynn could see he was about to finish.

"I thought you might want some lunch. Care for some company?"

"Sure, that would be great. This needs to dry before I can paint it."

Lynn spread the lunch on the table while Ray poured them each a mug of coffee.

"I don't know what I ever expected Wyoming to be like, but this wasn't it. It's amazing."

"You aren't bothered by the storm? I would think a guy from down south would find the cold and snow unpleasant."

"You would think, wouldn't you? I guess you'd be right about most people. I think it's amazing. I could live up here."

"So, why don't you? What's stopping you?"

"Well, I need to get to Dallas. My friend is depending on me. After that, who knows? Maybe, if I had a job waiting here I would be back."

The comment wasn't wasted on Lynn. Maybe, she thought, he was more than someone passing through.

"You mean, something like a motel handyman?"

Ray paused before answering, "That would work. I think that would work real well."

Lynn found herself blushing under Ray's gaze. To change the subject, she said, "Your van was parked under a tree and I was afraid a branch would fall on it. I moved it to another parking spot. I hope that was okay."

Ray hesitated and avoided looking at her before smiling and saying, "Thanks. That was very thoughtful. It's a rental and I sure would hate it if something happened to it."

§§§§§

Lynn was no fool. She had had enough men lie to her to know when one was hiding something. Whatever Ray was carrying in that van, he didn't want her to know about it. She knew it wasn't any of her business, but every time she saw the van she couldn't help but think about it.

She tried to distract herself by working on some paperwork. When she realized she had been staring at some forms for several minutes without reading a single word, she made up her mind. She wasn't going to be able to do anything until she knew what was going on. How had this guy gotten under her skin like that? He was only passing through, she reminded herself again. Or, was he? She had felt a strong reaction when he hinted he might be interested in staying.

He said he started in Idaho, she thought. Maybe he was carrying a load of illegal weapons to the Aryan Nations. If they were going to talk about him staying, she needed to know for sure. Grabbing the van keys, she didn't even bother putting on her coat.

Ray was looking out the window, gauging the storm, when he saw Lynn heading for the van. Dropping what he was doing he ran out the door as fast as he could but he couldn't stop her before she had climbed in the van. The passenger window was still covered with snow and he couldn't see what was happening inside, but he could guess.

"Oh, man. I'm dead," he thought before realizing the poor choice of words.

Lynn saw the strange bundle covered up by the blanket and pulled it back to see what was underneath. The air in the van was as cold as the subzero air outside but it suddenly seemed a lot colder. She calmly put the blanket back and left the van, locking the door as she did so.

Ray rushed up telling her, "Now, don't freak out! It's okay. It isn't what it looks like."

She looked at him and began to pull away.

"It looks like you have a dead guy in the back of your van! How is it not what it looks like?"

"He died from cancer. I was taking him home and he died during the trip. That's all there is to the story."

"You've been sitting here all this time with a dead guy in your van!?"

"Well, yeah. I didn't think you'd want me dragging him into the room. Besides, he's frozen solid. Nothing's going to harm him now."

"You've been sitting here all this time with a dead guy in your van?"

Ray was a little confused. "I thought we already went over that. He had cancer and I was taking him home to Dallas. He died on the way. Now, I can't get through because of the blizzard. What was I supposed to do?"

"Call the police! Take him to the hospital!"

"The insurance company won't pay unless I deliver him to the hospital in Dallas."

"What? A few hundred dollars for the van rental? I tell you what, I'll pay it, if that's all it is."

"It's over a hundred thousand dollars."

"What are you talking about?"

"He had a stroke in Idaho and was in a private hospital there. The insurance company won't pay for any of his hospital expenses unless I can get him to Dallas. A hundred thousand is a low-end guess. It's probably a lot more than that."

"You're telling me they're holding a dead man for ransom?"

"No. He has to be alive when I deliver him. Listen, it's really cold out here. Can we talk about this inside?"

"I'm not letting you back in until I know what's going on! If he has to be alive when you get him to Dallas it sure looks like you're out of luck."

"No. He'll be alive when I get him there."

"Oh, really! Who are you? Jesus Christ? You're going to raise him from the dead when you get to Dallas?"

"I'll just tell them he was alive when I arrived."

"What are you going to say, that he died just as you were pulling up? That has to be the dumbest damn plan!!!! You don't think doctors can tell the difference between a guy who just died and someone that's frozen like a popsicle?"

"I'll thaw him out before we get there."

"And, then what? You don't think they can tell he's been dead?"

"You got a better idea?"

"Yes! Let the hospital eat the cost."

"They won't eat it. They already said they'll come after Roger's estate. That's his name, by the way. Roger Tucci."

"Was his name."

"Is. He's still alive, remember. Until the doctors say otherwise."

"Who cares if they come after his estate? It isn't your problem."

"There's no money in the estate. They'll go after his power-of-attorney and she's a friend of mine. She's helped me out a bunch of times. She's been good to me. They'll take everything she has. I'm not going to do that to her."

"So, you're going to commit a felony by transporting a dead body across state lines and commit insurance fraud? Oh, and let it sit in my parking lot! What an idea! That is some good friend. Are you sleeping with her?"

91

"Why does everyone keep asking me that? No, I'm not sleeping with her. She's married and has two kids. She works part-time at a nursery and gets me work. She saved my life once. I made her a promise I would do this for her and I'm not going to let her down."

Lynn threw her arms up in the air in exasperation. "Come on in. Let's talk about this. This has to be just the dumbest damn thing I have ever heard of."

Her boots crunched in the snow as she led the way back to the office. She turned to look at him and asked, "She saved your life?"

"Yeah, it's a pretty good story, too."

"Oh, it better be."

§§§§§

"Five or six years ago, I met this girl, Dorothy, while I was living in Austin. We were doing pretty good when she decided to move back to Cisco. That's where she was from and she wanted to be closer to her parents and friends. Like I said, we were doing pretty good and I just did handyman work, so I went with her. Dorothy got a job at a nursery and I did odd job work around town. Together, we found a little house out in the countryside to rent and we were pretty happy."

They were sitting in Lynn's living room. She had poured him a hot mug of coffee to help warm up after standing out in sub-zero weather and he had his hands wrapped around it to absorb the heat.

"One day, we were out back in the yard and she pointed at this tree that had all of these flowers on it and she said, 'That's a hibiscus. I learned about them at the nursery. They say you can make tea from the flowers.' I thought this sounded pretty cool and we gave it a try. You're supposed to let the flowers dry out, but we tried them fresh and they worked and the tea was really good. I found out later they make it in Mexico and you can buy it in the stores.

"We picked a bunch of flowers and dried them out so we would have a supply. One day, Dorothy went to work and I didn't have anything going on so I was by myself at home. I went to make myself a cup of hibiscus tea but we were all out. I went to the tree and it still had some flowers so I picked a bunch of them. What I didn't notice was that I also picked these flowers from another plant at the same time. They were growing together and I didn't realize they were two different plants. Well, I took the flowers in and made tea with some and put the others out to dry.

"I drank the tea and went to work on some things around the yard. After working for a while I started feeling a little weird. I looked up and there was this unicorn standing there looking at me."

"A unicorn? Really!"

"Yeah. Just like from a movie. It was all white and graceful and had this big, beautiful horn coming out its forehead." He made a motion with his hand indicating something coming out of his forehead. "The weird part is I didn't really think it was all that strange a unicorn should be in my yard. I was like wondering if it had strayed over from the neighbor's or something. Then, it asked me the time."

"Come on. I thought this was a serious story. Next you're going to tell me it said it was late for a party."

"Hang on. Like I said, the unicorn asked me what time it was. It sounded like a man's voice, in a horse kind of way." He imitated a horse sound as he said, "'Do you know what time it is?' I checked my watch and said it was almost lunch time and Dorothy would be home soon. I told him Dorothy would like to meet him and asked if he would stay. Instead of answering me, he turned and walked away. I was watching him as he crossed the field when I realized my heart was going crazy. It was beating like I had run a hard race. I began to feel sick and started to head back to the house and that's the last thing I remember until I woke up in the hospital."

"What happened? Was it the tea?"

"Yeah, the other flower. Dorothy came home for lunch and she brought this friend, Patricia Kennealy, from the nursery with her. They found me on the ground in convulsions and called 911. When the emergency guys got there they said I was on an acid trip. They had seen it before they said, but Dorothy told them I don't do acid. They didn't listen to her and just went about their business. After they took me to the hospital, Dorothy and her friend went in the house to get some things for me before following. While Dorothy was in the bedroom Patricia was waiting in the kitchen and saw the flowers I had put aside to dry. When she realized what they were, she checked the sink and found the tea leaves from my tea. When Patricia asked about it, Dorothy told her where we got the flowers. Patricia had Dorothy take her to the tree and she took a close look. She told Dorothy there was a plant called Jimsonweed growing in the hibiscus and I had mixed some of the flowers in my tea. Turns out the Jimsonweed flower is a hallucinogenic. The Indians used to use it in rituals. It's also poisonous. I had used enough in my tea to kill me. Patricia took the flowers and the tea leaves to the hospital and showed them to the doctor there and explained what I did. Once they knew what was going on they were able to change the treatment. They told me later on they had been giving me the wrong treatment until Patricia told them about my mistake. If she hadn't found those flowers I would have died."

"Okay, you're right. That's a pretty good story. No side effects?"

"Nope. Made a full recovery. Except, you know, I still have dreams of that unicorn. How many guys do you know can say they had a unicorn ask them for the time?"

She laughed at his question. "None that I know of. What about Dorothy?"

"We split up after a couple of years. The house was in her name so I had to move out. She eventually moved back to Austin. I guess she didn't like being close to family after all. I liked it in Cisco and decided to stay. Patricia got me on the call list at the nursery for when they needed someone and I became a regular contract worker there. When Dorothy kicked me out, Patricia helped me find a place to live. She's always been real good to me. Kind of like a big sister. When she came to me for help and told me what she needed, I thought it was insane and had decided to tell her 'no.' But, when I opened my mouth I mysteriously said 'yes.'"

"And now here you are. With a dead body in my parking lot."

"Yeah, here I am. With a dead man in your parking lot. Except, he's not dead. I flew up to Idaho Falls and Patricia arranged for the rental van. The hospital couldn't get him out of there fast enough. They were actually waiting on the curb when I drove up. Assholes. They gave me about ten minutes of training on how take care of Roger and away we went."

"How long did you know him?"

"Had never laid an eye on him before I arrived at the hospital."

"When did he die?"

"Only a few hours after I picked him up. I stopped at a gas station in Pinedale and he was okay before I went in. When I came back a few minutes later he was gone. Just like that."

"And you decided to keep going to Dallas."

"I promised Patricia I would get him there. I have a lot of faults, but I keep my promises."

"How far is it to Dallas from here?"

"About 20 hours of driving, including stops. I don't think I can make that non-stop. I'll have to pull over and get some sleep somewhere."

"You're going to sleep in the van with a dead guy?"

"What else? I don't want to take the chance someone will find him in the back. It wasn't very pleasant the last time that happened."

"Have you told your friend about what happened?"

"No. He's alive as long as I'm the only one who knows. If I get into trouble, she can honestly say she knew nothing about it."

"Except, now I know about it. That makes me an accomplice before the fact."

"No, you don't know anything. I never told you about Roger and you never looked in the back. If anyone asks, that's what I'll tell them. This isn't your problem and I'm sorry I got you mixed up in it. Really, really sorry."

She sat silently glaring at him.

"Does that mean I get to stay?" he asked.

"I'm crazy to say it, but yes, you can stay. Besides, the roads should be open by tomorrow."

"In that case, I better get busy on that job. I don't want to run off and leave something unfinished." With that, he went back to the room, grateful he was able to get out of there without her calling the police.

After he left, Lynn sat there staring into her coffee. "I'm smarter than this. What the hell am I thinking?"

§§§§§

Ray worked through the afternoon. Not wanting to push his luck, he avoided Lynn as much as possible. Every time he completed a task, he crossed it off the list and enjoyed the feeling. It wasn't just the joy of accomplishment; he also enjoyed the idea of doing something nice for Lynn. Changing washers in leaky faucets might not sound romantic to some people, but it was what he could do.

The light outside was fading and he was busy fixing the wiring on a broken light when she showed up and stood silently watching, not returning his greeting. He continued his work under her watchful gaze until he finished and tried the lamp. He smiled when the light came on and marked another item off the to-do list.

Finally, he turned to her with a feeling of dread.

"You've been quiet. What's up?"

"Go change. I'll take you out to dinner."

That was about the last thing he expected her to say.

"By the way, we're taking my truck."

§§§§§

The snow was letting up and they passed snowplows on the way, but the streets were already mostly clear.

"Is it normally this busy on a Saturday night?" he asked. He had noticed how much traffic there was and thought of how empty the roads had been when he drove in the previous night.

"Well, it's normally pretty busy, but a lot of people are getting out after being cooped up for two days. Can you blame them?"

"No, but I'd have thought people up here were used to it."

"This was a pretty unusual storm. We get snow, but normally not so much at one time. Here we are," she said as they parked, pointing at the restaurant across the street.

The Coyote Creek Steakhouse and Saloon. The name by itself said volumes.

"It looks pretty fancy," he said as they got out.

96

"This is the best restaurant in Rock Springs. It's nice, but not so nice you can't wear jeans. I've been here when it has been excellent and I've been here at times when it was only so-so. It has great atmosphere and good service, and I really like this old building. Besides, parking is easy."

Ray opened the front door for her and followed her in to find the room crowded. There was a bar to one side and a large fireplace with a fire burning.

"I made reservations, so we're fine. This used to be a bank building. If you have a large party, you can sit in the old vault. It's pretty private in there."

They followed the waitress to their table and accepted menus after sitting down. Ray looked at the menu and was a little uncomfortable. Finally, he asked Lynn, "You've been here before. What do you recommend?"

"I'm planning on a burger. They're great! The Pepper Jack Chicken Sandwich is also good. The baby back ribs are good, as are the steaks. But, the veggies aren't always the best. But, basically, everything on the menu is good. This place isn't New York City quality, but it's still nice. Try the microbrew beers. They're good, too."

They engaged in small talk until they placed their orders. Once the waitress left, Ray asked her, "I see notes about this being 'historic downtown Rock Springs.' What's so historic about it?"

"There's a lot of history here, mostly from the railroads and mining. Not all of its good, though."

"This is the American West," he said. "There were some things done that shouldn't have been done."

"Yes, but there was an event here that was rough even for the American West. This is big coal mining country. In the 1880s, the mining company was replacing the white miners with cheaper Chinese workers. The area we're in now was the local Chinatown in the 1880s and was the location of one of the worst race riots in the country's history. In 1885, the white miners beat up some of the Chinese miners and walked off the job. That started things, and by the end of the day at least 28 Chinese workers were dead, although 50 is considered to be a better estimate. It was really horrible. The white miners came with rifles from multiple directions. Scouts went ahead to warn the Chinese they had an hour to get out of town, but within 30 minutes, people had already been shot dead. The Chinese people were running for their lives, but the white miners would chase them down as they tried to escape and beat and rob them. Any Chinese who resisted got shot. Later, the rioters set fire to the Chinese people's houses, burning people to death inside their homes. Even the women got into the act and shot at the fleeing Chinese. Chinese people were scalped, mutilated, branded, decapitated, dismembered and hanged from roofs."

"That's horrible! What happened to the rioters?"

"Some were arrested, but the grand jury said there was no testimony linking any of the arrested men to any crimes and refused to indict them. Everyone was released and returned home to a hero's welcome."

"Didn't anyone do anything?"

"Not much. There was a real fear in China that the people there would take revenge on Americans in the country, but nothing happened. It strained relationships between the U.S. and China for years. The workers' union refused to represent the miners here after that and, eventually, they all lost their jobs. Small consolation for what happened. The whole region suffered for years. Businesses and people didn't want to have anything to do with the town. They eventually closed the mine, although it took some time. The white people thought some of them might lose their mining jobs to the Chinese. Instead, they all lost their jobs, even non-miners. They failed to do the right thing and it came back to bite them. Karma's a bitch, as they say. You have to wonder what would have happened if they had learned to work together instead of hating and fighting. So, now you know the dark side of Rock Springs' history."

"Well, I think it looks like a nice town now. A nice, quiet place to live."

"It is. There's enough going on to keep it from getting boring, but not so much it gets hectic. A city person would go crazy here, but this is a good place if you want a simpler way of life."

"Compared to Cisco, this is a major metropolis. I know how to do the simple lifestyle."

He paused while trying to put the words to his thought.

"It's strange, when you think about it. Because Roger decided to hook up with an old girlfriend, I end up in Rock Springs and met you. How many things had to happen just right for that to happen? If it hadn't been for the storm I would've driven straight through. I might not have even noticed your motel."

"It's hard to know what your actions will lead to," she said. "I knew this guy even less than you and his decisions have still affected me."

They continued talking over their dinner and it was getting a little late by the time they left. Ray noticed Lynn was a little wobbly as they made their way back to her truck.

"Are you okay to drive?"

"Yeah, I'm fine. I only had three beers. That isn't much."

"Why don't you let me drive?"

Lynn looked at him with a smile and handed him the keys.

"Sure," and she climbed into the passenger side.

She leaned over in his direction a little as she gave him directions back to the motel, allowing her hand to rest on his arm at one point.

"Would you like to come in for some coffee," she asked after Ray parked the pick-up truck.

He looked at her and her beauty made him ache. He wanted to go with her badly, but it didn't feel right to him. This wasn't a one-night-stand kind of woman.

"No, thank you. I need to get a good night sleep. I have a long drive tomorrow."

"That's a good idea. I wouldn't want you falling asleep on the way back to Texas."

"The police might find the accident scene a little strange. Thanks for the offer, though. And, thank you for the dinner. I had a great time."

"I did, too. Good night, Ray."

"Good night, Lynn. I'll see you in the morning. Don't worry about breakfast. I'll get something after I'm on the road."

After he left, Lynn walked to her apartment without a hint of wobble.

Well, that was interesting, she thought.

§§§§§

It was clear and sunny when he got up the next morning and made his way to the office. Lynn was already waiting for him in the office.

"Well?" he asked.

"The road is open. You should get going before Roger gets impatient," she said as she handed him an envelope.

"What's this?"

"Your wages, minus the cost for your room."

"That wasn't the deal. You don't owe me anything."

"I know. But you worked hard and did a good job. You delivered more than you needed to. I like to keep business straight. You earned that money."

He stuffed the envelope in his coat pocket.

"Thank you, Lynn. For everything."

"Hey, if you ever get the urge for some cleavage to look at, come on back."

He laughed before saying, "No. I wouldn't come all this way for cleavage. But, I might come back for you."

On impulse, he bent forward and kissed her. She kissed back.

"Wow!" he said. "Great lips. Take care."

"Let me know how it goes," she said as he was leaving. She stood there and watched until he drove away. With a sigh, she thought out loud, "The nice ones always leave."

§§§§§

The air was cold but the highways were clear, and Ray made good time. Going east to Cheyenne, he turned south onto I-25, passing through Denver and Colorado Springs and on into New Mexico. In Raton he left the interstate and took U.S. Highway 87 to the southeast – towards Texas. About ten miles past Clayton he spotted a sign marking the start of the Central Time Zone. Less than a mile further was a large sign with a big Lone Star flag and the words, "Welcome to Texas. Drive Friendly - The Texas Way." Ray breathed a sigh of relief. He still had a long way to go before he reached

100

Dallas, but at least he didn't have to worry about transporting a body across any more state lines.

Reaching Dalhart at sunset, he filled up the gas tank and stopped at a diner along the highway for something to eat. His body ached from driving all day and he was glad to stretch his muscles as he made his way to a booth. He felt the envelope Lynn had given him that morning in his coat pocket and opened it. Inside were five $20 bills and a piece of paper with a phone number.

§§§§§

Including stops, it had been a twelve-hour drive from Rock Springs to Texas. Once he crossed over into Texas, it was another six-hour drive to Dallas plus stops. The highways blurred together in the darkness and all Ray could think about was the droning of the tires on the road. Passing through Amarillo and cutting across northern Texas, he reached Wichita Falls after midnight. He was tired and wanted to stop for some sleep, but he checked the schedule and realized if he stopped now he would hit the Dallas-Fort Worth Metroplex at rush hour. The thought made him decide to continue on, finally reaching Fort Worth a little after two in the morning. Exhausted from the long day, he found a secluded area off the highway where he could park. Reclining the driver's seat as far as it would go, he was asleep in moments.

It was still dark when he woke up, feeling a little confused about where he was. Collecting his wits, he turned and saw Roger's blanket-covered body and recalled what he was doing. He checked the time and saw it was nearly six o'clock. Still tired, but somewhat refreshed, he got back on the highway in an attempt to get through the Metroplex before traffic got too bad.

Ray called over his shoulder, "We're on the home stretch now, Roger. A couple more hours and we'll be there."

It took a little more than an hour to get through the two cities at that time of day and reach I-35 in Dallas going north towards the University of Texas Southwestern Medical Center. He exited the highway at Harry Hines and followed the signs towards the Medical Center, passing by Parkland Hospital, made famous on that dark day in

November, 1963 when President Kennedy was taken there after being shot. He drove until he was close to the Medical Center and pulled off the road, parking in an isolated area while he made a phone call.

"Patricia, it's Ray."

"Thank goodness. I've been worried sick, Ray. We were calling the highway patrol to find out if you had been in an accident. Why didn't you call? Where are you?"

"I'm near the Medical Center in Dallas. I need you to call Roger's doctor and have him meet us when I arrive."

"Is everything alright? What took you so long?"

"Everything's fine. We got held up by a blizzard in Wyoming."

"You sound like there's a problem. How's Roger?"

"No, no problems. I'm tired, is all. Roger is sleeping. The morphine does a number on him. But, you need to call the doctor and have him meet us. It's really important for him to meet us. Call me back after you've talked to him, okay?"

Ray sat there, feeling the weariness of the drive, waiting for Patricia to call back. He had terrible cottonmouth and dug in his bag to find his toothbrush, taking advantage of the wait to brush his teeth. Feeling refreshed, he reclined the seat to relax. The phone woke him when the call came in.

"Hello? Patricia?"

"Yeah, it's me. It took a while, but I was able to get hold of Dr. Takahashi. He told me there is a drive-up area right off Harry Hines where he'll meet you in twenty minutes. Will that work?"

"Yes. I'll call you after I'm done there."

He patiently watched the clock until enough time had passed. Then, putting the van in drive, he pulled onto the road and made his way to the Medical Center.

"This is it, Roger. Keep your fingers crossed."

When he arrived at the location he got out and looked around, feeling very nervous about what he was doing. Just as he was starting to get afraid the doctor wouldn't show up an Asian man wearing a doctor's white coat approached him.

"Dr. Takahashi?"

"Yes. Are you the one who brought Roger Tucci?"

"Yeah, Ray Krieger. He's in the back of the van. He's in pretty bad shape doctor. I thought you would want to take a look before we decide how to proceed from here." With that he opened the back door and the two of them climbed in. The doctor took one look and said, "This man's dead!"

"No, I think you're mistaken doctor. I was just talking to him. Take another look."

"Are you kidding?" he asked as he felt Roger's forehead. "He's cold as ice. He's not only dead, he's been dead for days."

"Doctor. Really. I don't want to tell you your business, but I don't think he's dead. I was talking to him just a few minutes ago."

"Did he talk back?"

"His speech was difficult by that time. Patricia told me you understood the situation. Take another look. Please."

Takahashi looked at Ray before turning back to the corpse, placing his hand on the side of Roger's neck.

"My apologies. You're right, I'm getting a pulse, but it's very weak. I don't think he's going to last much longer."

Takahashi sat there pressing his fingers against Roger's neck for a couple of minutes before announcing.

"He's gone." Pulling a piece of paper from his pocket he checked his watch and wrote the time down. "It appears your efforts were for nothing, Mr. Krieger. He barely made it here."

"I'm sorry to hear that. Thank you for your help doctor."

As the orderlies removed Roger from the van, Ray called Patricia and broke the news. Then, he found the phone number that had been in the envelope Lynn had given him and called her.

"Bad news," he said. "He died right after we arrived."

"I'm sorry to hear that. Thanks for letting me know."

"Sure. But, there's something else I wanted to talk to you about. I've had a lot to time to think. Is that job offer still good?"

§§§§§

103

Ray was sitting on the front porch, staring out into space, when Patricia drove up.

Oh, great! she thought. *Stoned already.*

The caliche gravel in the dirt driveway crunched as she approached. Ray watched but didn't make any effort to acknowledge her.

"Hello, Ray. How are you?"

He tilted his head to one side and gave her a smile.

"Mrs. K! How are you? What brings you out this-a-way?"

"I wanted to see how you're doing and tell you how much I appreciate what you did."

He turned and looked her in the eyes. She could see he was completely sober.

"You're welcome. I'm glad I was able to help. It was a real experience. How did it work out with the insurance company?"

"They're pissed. They think it's very suspicious Roger died right after getting to the hospital after almost three days on the road, but there's nothing they can do about it. Roger's instructions were that he wanted to be cremated right away. That means there's no body for an autopsy. Now, they say they won't pay all of the hospital charges and the hospital is threatening to sue them if they don't. They're fighting like cats and dogs. It couldn't have happened to a better group of people. I hope it does go to court. That's one hearing I would love to see. In any event, the estate is covered. Meaning, I'm covered."

Ray had a quiet smile as he listened. Patricia actually found it unsettling.

"What's up Ray?"

"I've decided to leave. I'm moving to Wyoming."

"Wyoming? Why in the world would you do that?"

"Someone told me to look at my options, throw out what I can't do and then it's easier to decide between what's left."

She rolled her eyes at his comment, "Oh, my god! He got to you!"

Ray continued to smile. "I have a job there. I'm going to work as the handyman at a motel."

Patricia gave him a hard look before answering, "There's a woman, isn't there? Is that why you're moving up there?"

Ray just gave her a bigger smile.

"I told someone recently I got stoned because I was waiting. I feel as if I'm not waiting anymore. There's something you can do for me, Patricia. I'm taking what I can in my car. Could you take care of the rest of my things? Sell what you can and give the rest away. Give the money to some charity. I don't care which one."

"Oh, Ray. Are you sleeping with her?"

"No. At least, not yet."

"All of this because I asked you to bring Roger home."

"Funny how that worked out. Who could have seen this a week ago?"

"Not I," she said, but she was thinking about ripples on a lake.

Interlude

Roger and Kristen were celebrating in style. Earlier, Roger had purchased a business that was about to shut down and had turned it around before selling it for a very handsome profit. It was Roger's biggest deal so far and Kristen was a happy wife as a result.

They had all of their friends over to their house and it was a boisterous crowd. Roger was pleased with the way things were going and was pleased to see one of his best friends was able to make it.

Neal Dent shook Roger's hand. "Congratulations on the sale, Roger. It was a very nice job you did there. Those people were going to be unemployed if it hadn't been for you."

"Thanks, Neal. That's one of the things that makes it work. Give people a chance to control their own destiny and they'll help you out. Of course, giving them a piece of the profit never hurts."

Neal shuffled his feet and kept glancing down at the floor.

"Listen, Roger, can we go somewhere private? I need to talk to you about something."

"Sure. Let's go to my study."

Once Roger closed the door he asked his friend, "Can I get you something to drink?"

"Thanks. A whiskey straight up would be fine."

Neal was looking at the books on the shelves, meandering around the room. Roger waited patiently, allowing Neal to collect his thoughts.

"How do you do it, Roger? How do you turn businesses around like that?"

"I look at the business, come up with every possible option and eliminate the things I can't do. Normally, there are only a few options remaining to decide on, sometimes only two or three. At that rate, even if I'm guessing, I have a thirty to fifty percent chance of succeeding. If you can be right with thirty percent of your decisions in business, you'll be a success."

"You make it sound easy."

106

"It isn't, but with practice you can get pretty good at it. The big trick is to figure out the things you can't do and then not worry about them anymore."

"Maybe that's what my problem is, I can't stop thinking about the things I can't do." He hesitated before continuing. "I'm in trouble, Roger. Big trouble."

Roger wasn't surprised. He had already surmised Neal needed help, probably of the monetary kind.

"How bad is it?"

"They'll take everything I own if I don't do something. They'll throw me in jail."

"What happened?"

Neal was nervously pacing as he talked. "I invested some clients' money in something I shouldn't have. I thought it was a sure-fire winner, but it went bust. I lost everything I put in. Now, I'll be facing embezzlement charges unless I can replace all of the money."

"How much are we talking about?"

He stopped pacing and ran a hand through his hair before taking a drink from his glass. "Nearly fifty thousand dollars."

"That's a lot of money, Neal."

"It was worse than that. I've already borrowed everything I can and cut the losses down. I've taken a home equity loan. I've cashed in all of our savings. We're broke, Roger, and I'm still short. Please, Roger. Can you loan me the money? I swear I'll pay back every cent. I just don't want to go to jail. Jane and the kids would be penniless. I don't know who else I can go to except you."

Roger didn't even hesitate. "Don't worry, Neal. I'll loan you the money."

Neal looked as if he was about to start weeping as he shook Roger's hand. "Thank you, Roger. You don't know what this means to me. I can't thank you enough."

"It's okay, Neal. We've been friends for a long time. I would hope you would do something like this for me."

"Of course I would. You know I would be right there with you."

"How soon do you need the money?"

"Right away. I don't know when they'll check the books, but it'll be within a few days."

"Alright then, just give me your bank information and we can do this right now."

Neal produced his checkbook and Roger used the information to make an electronic transfer. Turning off the computer monitor, Roger said, "There you go. You've got the money. You and your family will be fine, now. But Neal, remember when I said I figured out the things I couldn't do? Well, embezzling money is one of the things I was talking about. Even if the investment had been a success, that's one of the things you can't do. Ever. Understand?"

"I know, I know. I don't know what came over me. I won't do it again, I promise. I've learned my lesson."

"Good. Now, let's go back to the party before we're missed."

Kristen approached him when they could speak privately.

"What were you and Neal talking about? You were gone a long time."

Roger told her about their conversation.

"What did you do?"

"I loaned him the money, of course."

"Oh, Roger! How could you do that without talking to me first?"

"Neal and I have been friends since elementary school. What was I supposed to do?"

"Let him go to jail," she said angrily. "That's what criminals are supposed to do!"

"And, what about Jane and the kids? And, what about all of those people whose money he took?"

"I'm sorry for them, but they aren't our problem! You can't solve all of the world's problems, Roger."

"No, I can't. But, I was able to solve this one."

"And, just how long is he going to take to pay it back?"

"I don't expect he ever will."

She nearly screamed before remembering there was a room full of people right next to them. "What? You knew this and you gave him the money? What an idiot! What a goddamn, stupid idiot!"

"Listen, Kris, I put up with a lot from you. You're my wife and I love you, but don't ever talk to me like that again. Just because we've been married 20 years doesn't mean you can treat me that way."

"Roger! You just gave away fifty thousand dollars! How did you think I would react?"

"I knew you would be this way and that's why I didn't talk to you first. We have plenty of money. We'll write it off on our taxes as a business loss. And, we still have more money than we need. I wasn't going to sit there with a fat bank account while one of my best friends loses everything he has."

Kristen stormed away without another word. By the time party ended she was quite drunk. It didn't help things and it was a long night for both of them.

Hung over, Kristen still managed to leave early the next morning to get out of the house and spend the day with her friends. Left alone, Roger went to a nearby favorite bakery for breakfast and was surprised to see the sign in the window announcing it was going out of business. He had met the owner before, so she didn't think it strange when he approached her and asked about her situation.

"We were doing real well and I borrowed heavily to expand. Then, the economy tanked and people stopped buying bakery goods. I don't have any more money. The only way I can handle my debt is to sell everything off. They'll come in and take it anyway if I don't."

Roger listened quietly. When she was done he said, "You are such a lovely woman. I hate to see you so upset. Just look at you frowning. You would look so much prettier with a smile." He had taken her hand in both of his and was looking her right in the eyes. She felt like she had been hypnotized and couldn't stop looking back. It was as if he had taken control of her emotions and she found herself smiling despite her situation. "There you go. That's so much better. Maybe I can help. That's what I do. I help businesses that are in trouble. I bet we can find something you haven't thought about. What time do you close today?"

"It's Saturday so we close early, right after lunch."

"Wonderful. Why don't we meet for a late lunch and discuss it?"

109

Without knowing why, she found herself nodding her head and agreeing on a time to meet.

Kristen was still mad when she returned that evening and it didn't help her attitude when she found Roger happily whistling.

"*Shit!*" she thought. "*That bastard got laid!*"

Roger assumed the business loans at the bakery in exchange for a majority ownership. With his help, they implemented a bike-riding home delivery system for the M-street area. Roger made sure there was plenty of press coverage for the unique service and, within six months, Roger's loans were paid off. Within a year, the owner was able to buy out Roger. It didn't come close to making up the money he gave to Neal, but it was enough to make Kristen happy.

Chapter Eight

When Patricia drove Ray to the airport for his trip to Idaho to bring Roger back, it had been her intent to continue to his office to comb through his records and find out what was going on. She was also hoping to find a bank account somewhere with more than $63. Instead, she found a diner and stopped for coffee and a Danish.

It was barely daybreak and she was already exhausted. In the last twenty-four hours she had disconnected Roger from life support, learned about his financial situation, flown back to Texas, talked to the insurance company and their lawyer before breaking the news to John, convinced Ray to go to Idaho after making all of the arrangements, and gotten up early to take him to the airport. It was no wonder she was tired. More like drained. She didn't know how much more she could go through. But, she knew she had to find a way to keep going.

Once in Roger's office, she had Jana show her where the business files were kept. She was going to have to dig through them until she understood the situation. She and Jana started with the filing cabinets filled with business files. Roger had kept excellent records over the years and there were files going back to when he first began. As they were going through the records Patricia had Jana divide them into two piles – those that were still going concerns and those that were closed. After several hours she was looking at a large pile of closed deals and only one, thin folder in the open deal stack.

Combined with the financials she had received, the picture she got was a depressing one. Roger had made, and burned through, millions of dollars over the course of his career. There were deals where he had made huge profits in mere months and others where he had lost almost his entire investment. But, the winners clearly outweighed the losers. The more she learned, the more she appreciated how good of a businessman Roger had been. She was also impressed with how neat his files were. She knew he was an unorganized slob most of the time.

But, what happened to all of the money?

A few bad investments, the divorce, gifts to his children, taking care of his mother, charities, and a lavish lifestyle accounted for much of it. Then, there were the

111

handouts. From what she could tell, everyone with a cause came to Roger for support and he didn't turn any of them away.

Still, what was he planning on using to pay the bills with? With the one exception, every deal she examined was over and that one was nothing more than a defaulted loan he had made to someone. There were no money-makers remaining.

"Jana, are there any files missing? I can't find any deals Roger was actively working on."

"The only thing I know he was still working on was MGC. He might have taken that file home with him before going to Idaho."

"What is MGC?"

"I don't know. He gave me some instructions to set up a PayPal account and I know he was working on a website. It was all very different than other business deals he's done. He was kind of secretive about it."

"You know, I have his keys. I brought his personal things back with me, so I'm going to go to his apartment and look for this file."

She ran what she had learned through her head during the drive to the Essex Apartments, and by the time she arrived she felt she was beginning to hope she might find something useful.

It hadn't really occurred to her what she was doing until she was standing in front of the door to the apartment. Then, it hit her. She was using his keys to enter his apartment and she was authorized to do it. She was authorized because he was nearing death and she had assumed control of his interests. A wave of grief hit her and she leaned against the door and wept.

After composing herself, she opened the door and found Roger's apartment was clean, but unorderly. She had seldom been in the apartment except for parties and dinners and it was all clean and neat those times. Now, it was the way Roger kept it from day to day. Maybe Roger could find things here, but she was having a hard time. Finally, on a lamp table next to a reading chair she found a thick file folder marked "MGC." With a sigh of relief, she sat in the chair and opened it up. On the first page, she read "Marijuana Growers Conference."

She closed the folder again and thought, "Oh, no! I'm going to jail."

The police were scowling at her in disgust. They led her to her cell, and as the iron door was closing it made a sound curiously like the ring tone on her phone.

She awoke confused, not knowing where she was at first. By reflex, she answered her phone without really thinking about what she was doing but noted it was John who was calling.

"Hi, honey. What's up?" she said groggily.

"That's what I was calling to ask you. What's going on? Are you coming home tonight?"

The stress had gotten to her and she had fallen asleep in the chair. She checked the time by a clock on the wall. It gave her a chance to get her bearings.

"It's getting late and I'm really tired. This has worn me out. I think I should stay here for tonight. I might be able to come home tomorrow."

"Have you found anything yet?"

"I found Roger was getting into the drug business."

"Whaaaat?"

She gave him a brief summary of what she had found.

"A conference to bring in marijuana growers?"

"It was supposed to be a chance for commercial growers to sell their ideas to a panel of investors. Roger had lined up these investors and was promoting the idea to the marijuana community. He was going to start a series of conferences and make money off the registration fees."

"Oh, man. You're going to jail."

"Thanks for the reassurance. I'll be sure to tell them you were in it with me. Maybe if we're both prisoners they'll give us twice as many conjugal visits. His and hers."

"I'm sorry. It was a joke. Don't worry. If there isn't any actual marijuana involved, they can't arrest you for talking about it."

"That's better. Still, I have to be concerned. John, I don't know how to handle this. I'm not a business woman. I don't know how to promote and manage a conference. It would be a lot better if I canceled the whole thing. I can't believe there would be that many people interested in it."

"Okay, if that's what you think. But, keep in mind you need to find a way to pay Roger's debts. Is there anything else he was involved in?"

"I haven't found anything, but his files are pretty extensive, so there might still be something."

"Well, sleep on it. You're stressed and you have a right to be with all you've been through. You can make your decision tomorrow when you're more rested. You need a good night's sleep before you do anything."

She agreed and they ended the call. Sitting alone in Roger's apartment made her feel surreal. Memories of her experiences with him came flooding back. It was strange, she thought, how he had seduced so many women and had so many business deals, but he turned to her to take care of him when he needed it most. Why not his children? Why not one of his other friends? Why didn't he at least ask one of his business partners to handle his affairs? What did he see in her that made him trust her so much?

One more time, she was struck by how Roger seemed to exist in a realm the rest of the world didn't see.

Interlude

Failure comes in many forms and they aren't all equal. Roger was use to the idea of failure, but this was one thing that didn't get easier with practice. And, this particular failure was harder than most. Normally, he would be able to recover something. Assets that could be sold or residual money in bank accounts. It was the exception where you lost everything. This was one of those times.

He finished reviewing the financials for the business and turned to Rudy Boland.

"Is this everything?" he asked. Frequently, people will hide a little money to cushion the fall.

"Yeah. That's it. There's nothing left."

Roger could see he was telling the truth. There were no hidden kitties of money. He got up and in a sudden burst of anger kicked a trash can across the room.

"How did this happen!? The quarterly reports showed you were doing well. Not great, but well enough to keep the doors open."

Boland stood nervously before answering.

"My partner, Laurence Gardin, died suddenly about six months ago. Things fell apart after that. I tried to make up for it, but I couldn't replace him. I quickly lost several contracts. It took a while for it to show up in the financials."

"How am I just now hearing about this?"

"I thought I would be able to pull everything together. It wasn't until he was gone that I fully understood how much Laurence brought to the partnership."

"So, you faked the financial reports. Let me guess, you knew I would pull the plug and you thought if you could go just another month things would turn around. Am I right?"

"No, I didn't fake them. I swear."

"What I don't understand is how you got everything past the CPA," he said, referring to how he always had a certified public accountant provide a quarterly report for each business deal.

Boland finally spoke up. "I didn't. The books for the last quarter were bad, but good enough. I simply delayed the most recent report, hoping you wouldn't ask about them before I had a chance to turn things around."

Roger filed that bit of news away for future reference. The reports were supposed to come straight to his office, not through the business being reviewed. One more loophole someone was able to find and use. Roger knew Boland ran a prior business into the ground before declaring bankruptcy. But, now he was partnered with Laurence Gardin. Boland was the brain behind the business while Gardin was the brain behind the marketing. He was the one who could land contracts and keep customers happy. Boland had none of those skills. Roger had been satisfied it was a good partnership when he invested in it. Again, he wondered how he was only hearing about Gardin's death now.

Roger understood what happened next. After Gardin died, Borland thought he would be able to do everything himself. When things started going bad, he convinced himself he could turn it around, he just needed a little more time. It was the mentality of a gambling addict. The next bet was going to be the big payoff. Just one more bet.

"This is what is going to happen. You'll cease operations immediately and close shop. I hate to see your employees lose their jobs like that, but there is no more money and I'm not going to give you any more. That would merely delay the inevitable. The next thing you'll do is to liquidate whatever assets you have."

"There aren't any. Everything is rented. Even the office furniture is rented."

"Fine. Call the owners and tell them to come collect their property. Is there anything you own outright?"

Rudy shrugged his shoulders and looked around the office with a glazed look.

"As far as I can think of, that painting is the only thing I have," he said, pointing to a line drawing of a woman carrying a fish. "I picked it up at an art show while on a business trip and paid cash for it. There's nothing special about it. I just liked it. I didn't even pay all that much for it. But I used company money so it belongs to the company."

Roger walked up to the picture and examined it for several seconds. Rudy could see Roger's face relax and he lost much of the stress he had been showing. For a moment, it seemed as if he was traveling to another place.

"Fine. Now it's mine," he said as he took it off the wall.

"I'll have an attorney contact you about liquidating the partnership. Tell everyone the bad news and go home, Rudy. You need to start looking for a new job."

With that, Roger walked out carrying the only asset he took from the investment.

Once he was back in his office he tried to relax and let go of the stress. Things hadn't been going well lately and this latest failure wasn't welcome news. He was going to have to find some good investments soon or he was going to follow Boland into bankruptcy. Looking at the simple painting helped him get control of his thoughts.

"I'm going to call you St. Raphaela," he told the painting.

He was gazing at it, lost in thought, when the phone rang.

"Roger? It's Neal. Listen, I'd like to discuss an investment opportunity with you. Can you come over?"

"Well, can you give me an idea of what it's about?"

Neal gave a quick description of the business deal and Roger had to admit it sounded promising.

"How much money are we talking about and where are you getting your part?"

"I'm going to invest my client's deposits. They'll get a huge payoff and I'll get a finder's fee. Roger, this deal has your name all over it."

"Neal, we discussed this before. You can't invest your clients' money without their approval. You know that. No, Neal. I can't do this with you. If you can find the money from a different source, I might be interested. But, I'm not going to get involved with embezzling."

The two men argued back and forth before Roger told his friend, "I'll tell you what I can do, Neal. Send me the particulars on the investment. If I think it's any good, I'll invest in it and pay you a finder's fee. That's the best offer I can make you. Are you interested?"

The other man was silent, but Roger waited patiently.

"Let me think about it. Okay?"

"That would be good. Call me back when you've reached a decision."

After he hung up, Roger thought about the two men he had dealt with today. Both men were repeating the same mistakes they had committed previously. Truly, he thought, the best indicator of future behavior was past behavior.

117

With that, Roger got a folder and opened a new business file. The only thing it contained was a single page of paper detailing the loan he had made to Neal when he had gotten in trouble before. When he was done he gave it to his secretary to file away.

He again found himself staring at the painting, St. Raphaela, thinking about how one of the partners in this investment had died and he hadn't heard about it. He would have to do something about that, but more importantly, what was he going to do about his own situation? His recent failures had made him think about the future. What if he died? What would happen to the company? What would happen to his family? He would need someone to manage things and he knew who he could trust. He was reaching for the phone to call his attorney but it rang before he picked it up.

"Okay, Roger. You have a deal."

"Great. Send me the particulars and we'll work up a finder's fee for you."

It turned out to be a great investment and ended Roger's string of failures. Roger forgot all about calling his attorney.

Chapter Nine

Patricia was a little sore after sleeping on Roger's couch, but a lot less stressed than the day before. She had spent the rest of the previous night enjoying Roger's excellent liquor cabinet, watching some television, and getting to bed early, sleeping on the couch. She had never slept in Roger's bed before and she wasn't about to start now. As she folded the sheet she had thrown on the couch, she thought she felt the best she had felt since this had all begun. John was right – a good night's sleep had done wonders. She felt ready to face the next challenge.

It didn't take long to arrive.

She was searching through his disturbingly empty refrigerator and cabinets for something to eat when there was a knock on the door. A man in his twenties was there when she answered.

"Sorry to bother you so early, ma'am. I'm looking for Mr. Tucci. We noticed someone was in the apartment. Is he home?"

"No, I'm sorry. He's out of town. I'm a friend of his. Can I take a message for him?" She didn't worry about the man's interpretation of 'friend.' It had happened many times over the years. She had gotten used to it.

"We were just wondering when we can expect him to pay his rent."

If he had asked last week she would have been confused, but not now.

"Give me directions to the office and I'll be there soon."

She had come across too many surprises in the last day for her to start getting upset now, she thought. After letting the young man go, she calmly went back to the kitchen and made a breakfast of Ranch Style beans, chocolate ice cream, and dried apricots.

"That was surprisingly good," she thought as she locked the apartment door.

When she arrived at the office she asked for the manager. He was there, despite it being Saturday morning, and she introduced herself.

"I'm Patricia Kennealy, I'm Mr. Tucci's legal guardian. I understand there's a problem with his rent."

The manager was a tall black man, clean shaven, portly, and well dressed. His shaved head reflected the light.

"Nice meeting you, Ms. Kennealy. I'm Preston Pickert. Please have a seat."

"Mrs. Kennealy."

"My apologies. I didn't mean any offense."

"None taken."

"You said 'legal guardian.' Is there a problem with Mr. Tucci?"

"Mr. Tucci is somewhere between here and Idaho. He had a massive stroke last week while he was up there taking care of some business. I'm his power-of-attorney agent and am authorized to act on his behalf."

"I'm very sorry to hear the news. He has been a good tenant and has been with us for many years. How is he doing?"

"He's dying. He has terminal cancer. I have someone bringing him home to die."

"Again, I'm very sorry. This must be a bad time for you. Would you prefer we talk about this later?"

"No, but thank you for the offer. I'm in town to take care of his business. The more I know about his affairs, the better. I'll do my best to take care of things. Based on what the man knocking on his door this morning said, I understand he's behind on his rent. Is that correct?"

He nodded in acknowledgement.

"The fact is, he's two months in arrears on his rent, nearly $4,500. Like I said, he's been a very good tenant and we've never had any problem with him before. The Essex Apartments has been glad to have him as a tenant. We are willing to work with you and I'm very understanding of his condition. I didn't know. Let me ask, will you be able to bring his account up to date?"

"No. He's completely broke and there's no money."

Pickert put his fingers together and thought for a few seconds before responding.

"I understand. How would you like to proceed?"

"I'm not sure. After what I've learned of the condition of his business affairs, this isn't a surprise, but it is unexpected. Can you give me a little bit of time to think about things and figure out what to do?"

"Of course. We're here to help any way we can. Here's my card. If you can keep us informed, we would appreciate it."

Patricia pocketed the card and thanked him for his understanding. As she walked to her car she thought of how this was just one more thing to resolve and wondered how many more surprises Roger had left for her to discover.

She was glad to see Jana was already at the office when she arrived on a Saturday morning. She was afraid the girl had already quit. She decided not to waste time. The poor girl had already been through too much. "Good morning, Jana. Can we talk?"

They went into the inner office and Patricia went to sit in Roger's chair, but hesitated. It was one more milestone she had to accept – assuming Roger's place in the office. Her emotions threatened to overwhelm her as she sat in Roger's chair with Jana sitting on the other side of the desk. She masked her tears by taking the time to run her hands over the leather of the fine chair and taking in the smell, then leaning forward to feel the surface of the desk. She could feel the fine indentations where Roger had pressed too hard while writing. Jana patiently waited without speaking. Finally, she spoke to Jana, keeping her eyes turned towards to the desk top.

"As you know, Roger is broke. I don't know how I'm going to pay your back salary, but I want to assure you I will do everything I can to see you get everything coming to you. Considering the situation, I would understand if you quit and moved on to another job. But, I would greatly appreciate it if you would stay and help. I don't know Roger's business and he is too far gone to advise me. I haven't even heard from him or Ray. I'm on my own, unless you help me."

"I really don't have a choice, do I? If I leave, I won't get my back pay. If I stay, I'm working on a gamble."

"No. Like I said, I promise my best to get you everything Roger owes you, even if you leave. I don't want you to think you have to stay to get what's yours. But, it will improve your chances if you do. I'm not going to lie to you, things are bad. Roger made a mess of things and I don't know business. I'm going to need help and you're the first person I'm turning to. Will you help?"

"I'll tell you what I'll do. I'm going to start applying for new jobs, but I'll stay here until I get something. Will that work?"

"That is more than I could ask for. Thank you, Jana. If you need a letter of reference, I'll be glad to write one. How long have you been working for him?"

"About five years. The lady before me had been with him for over twenty years. It was pretty tough learning the way he does things. He does a lot in his head. But it went smoothly after I learned the ropes. I'll miss him."

Patricia was surprised to learn she was old enough to have been with Roger five years. She looked as if she was in her late teens or early 20s.

"So will I," she said. "Now, let me tell you what I've learned."

Patricia brought her up to date on what she knew about MGC.

"I'm not prepared to handle a conference. My thought is to cancel the conference and close up shop. We'll sell the assets and try to pay off all of Roger's debts."

"But, what about all of the money in the PayPal account?" asked Jana.

Patricia shook her head before asking, "What money?"

"We have a bunch of people already registered."

She was surprised by the news, but discounted it. "We'll refund it. It can't be that much."

"$30,000."

"Okay, that got my attention. What are you talking about?"

"It's from the registration fees. The registration period is still open, so we may get more."

"Why didn't you tell me about this?"

"I did. It was right there in the financials." Jana got a copy of the financial statements from her desk and returned to Patricia. "See? It's right there under 'Continuing Operations.' But, he also made contracts for the conference totaling about $45,000. If you cancel the contracts you'll still have to pay some of them, but you won't have any money. Right now, there's money but not enough to cover expenses. We need to get more people to register before it can break even. Roger was very secretive about this account so I didn't know what you were talking about before. But after what you said the pieces fell in place. I can also tell you this – the registration money is going into an escrow account. You can't touch any of it until there's enough to pay the contracts. I thought that was a strange setup, but it kind of makes sense now."

Patricia took some time to let this new development sink in.

Jana sat quietly before finally asking, "What do you want to do?"

"Do? I'll tell you what we're going to do. We're going in the cannabis growing business!"

§§§§§

"I'm a little worried about Ray," she told John. "He was supposed to get Roger Friday afternoon. It's been two days and it's only a one-day drive. If he was able to stay ahead of the storm, he should have made it to Dallas by now. I tried calling, but I didn't get an answer. Do you think he might have had an accident?"

"It's possible. The storm was bigger and faster than the forecast said. If he got caught, there's no telling what might have happened. My guess is he had to hole up somewhere while the storm passed and hasn't been able to get through to you. I know someone with the highway patrol. I'll see if he can find out anything. What about you, are you coming home? It's going to get cold when that storm moves in."

"I brought a coat and I'm staying at Roger's apartment. I'll be fine. I need to get through all of his finances to find out what the story is. Jana was here with me yesterday and she's been a big help, but it's been more involved than I thought. Tomorrow's Monday, so I'll be able to contact some people."

"Okay. Let me know if there's anything I can do."

She thanked him before ending the call and rested her head for a few moments. She hadn't wanted to tell her husband she already knew what the story was – Roger had been in serious debt. Between the conference, Jana's back pay, the overdue rent on the apartment and the office, car payments, credit cards, and more, Patricia had already figured Roger was more than $50,000 in debt. After factoring in the MGC, she estimated Roger was at least $65,000 short. The conference would have to be a roaring success to pay it all off.

§§§§§

123

When the caller ID on her phone said Ray was calling Monday morning, Patricia nearly jumped at the phone in her anxiety to hear any news. Ray told her he was approaching the hospital and asked her to get hold of Dr. Takahashi to meet them. He told her Roger was sleeping, but she thought there was something wrong. Instead of pursuing the issue, she did as he asked and arranged for the doctor to meet Ray and Roger. She was so relieved to hear they were all right that she didn't push too hard for answers.

Then, she waited.

Sitting quietly, with her hands folded in her lap, an onlooker would never have guessed at the turmoil she was experiencing. When Ray called again, she was quite composed as she answered. For some reason, she was expecting the news and when he told her Roger had died at the hospital she was able to calmly thank him and tell him she would call back.

Then, she put her head in her hands and cried.

§§§§§

After calling Roger's family, she broke the news to Jana and John, letting them both know she was picking Ray up at the rental return and taking him back to Cisco. Jana didn't know just how bad Roger's condition was and she didn't take the news very well.

On the way back to Cisco, Patricia finally worked up the nerve to ask Ray, "Why did you need Dr. Takahashi to meet you? Why couldn't it be whoever was on duty?"

"Roger was in bad shape, Mrs. K. I thought it would be best if his doctor saw him in case he needed something special."

"How was Roger, Ray? I mean, you guys were together for almost three days. How did things go?"

"It was fine. He didn't need much taking care of. He was asleep most of the time."

"I was really worried. John called the highway patrol to see if you had been in an accident."

124

"The storm caught us and they closed the highways. We had to stop for the weekend."

"Where did you stay?"

"Rock Springs, Wyoming. Listen, Mrs. K, I would be glad to tell you the whole story, but I drove all night long and I'm really tired."

"I know and I'm sorry to ask you all these questions, I'm simply wondering why you didn't call me with an update. That's all."

"My phone died. I forgot my charger."

"And, it miraculously recharged itself this morning?"

Ray turned to her and said, "Listen, Patricia. Suppose I did something, something I could get into trouble for. And, if I were to tell someone else about it, then they could get into trouble also. I'm not saying I did anything wrong. I'm just saying there could be all sorts of reasons why someone might not give an update. I might ask why you didn't rush to the hospital to meet us. Instead, you sat and waited for me to call you back. You're not the 'sit and wait' kind. So, someone might ask why you did. You know what I mean?"

Patricia nodded her head. "I understand. Why don't you take a nap now."

In fact, she understood everything Ray wasn't telling her. She figured she probably understood all along, she merely needed confirmation.

Once she was home after dropping Ray off at his cabin, she called up Dr. Takahashi. He was with a patient and she had to leave a message asking him to call her. Then, once again, she quietly waited, sitting in the dim room with her hands folded in her lap. When he finally called, she felt very calm.

"Doctor, I'm calling about Roger's body. Is it still at the hospital?"

"Yes. We haven't received any instructions yet. Is that why you're calling?"

"Yes. I was wondering if it will be necessary to do an autopsy."

"No. He was terminally ill and he died in my care, so no autopsy is required. I already signed the death certificate. I assumed you would want to take care of him quickly"

Reading between the lines only confirmed the impression she got from Ray's comments. "Yes. It was Mr. Tucci's wishes to have his body cremated as soon as possible after he died. Would it be possible to have his body released to a funeral home?"

"As soon as you would like."

"Wonderful. I'll have someone there today."

After making arrangements with a funeral home, Patricia poured herself a glass of wine and relaxed.

I sure am tired, she thought. *I think I'll call the insurance company tomorrow to tell them the news. Maybe even Wednesday. Yeah, Wednesday would be better.*

§§§§§

It was quiet in the Kennealy household that evening as the idea of Roger's death sunk in.

Patricia was now the executor of Roger's will and she had brought it home with her to review but hadn't looked at it yet. John was giving it a quick run through for her when he stopped to reread one part closely.

"Did you see this about his funeral arrangements?"

"No, I haven't read any of it."

"He asked for you to do a memorial service. He specifically says he wanted you to do it."

"Oh, great. I was hoping his children would do that."

"It gets better."

"What do you mean?"

John handed her the papers and she read where he indicated. Then, she read it again. Finally, she sat back and looked at him.

"This is the gift that just keeps giving."

Interlude

The painting was prominently displayed, so Patricia had noticed it before, but had never looked closely until now. It was of a line drawing, done in purple, of a woman wearing a cloak and carrying a fish. It was quite simple with little detail, but beautiful at the same time.

Roger stepped next to her and lifted his glass as a small salute to the painting.

"Is there a story here?" she asked.

"No, not really. I got it as a result of a business deal gone bad. I call it St. Raphaela."

"That one doesn't sound familiar. Who is she?"

"Well, there is no Saint Raphaela. The real saint is Raphael, one of the archangels. But, I thought she fit the description. Besides, if archangels can appear as a man, why can't they appear as a woman?"

"Why the fish?"

"Ah! That goes to the story of Raphael, Tobias and Sarah. A different Sarah. Not the Sarah you're thinking of. As the story goes, Tobias was traveling the road to Media when he met a man, Azariah, who agreed to travel with him. When they got to Media, Azariah introduced Tobias to Sarah and told him he needed to marry her. Tobias wasn't thrilled with this idea because he knew Sarah was cursed. She had been married seven times and all seven times her husbands had been killed by a demon before the marriage could be consummated."

"Poor Sarah, a seven-time widow and still a virgin. How do we know she wasn't a nervous bride that was offing her husbands when they tried to put their hands on her?"

"Because the Bible says it was a demon. Don't get too literal. Anyway, Azariah tells Tobias he needs to spend each of the first three nights with Sarah praying to God and this will free her of the curse. So, they get married and in the morning Sarah's father digs a grave for Tobias. But, when he goes in, he finds Tobias is still alive and the two of them are praying. This goes on for two more nights and then they live happily ever after."

127

"Sounds to me that three days was enough for her to get used to the idea of having sex instead of killing him in private. It's an interesting story, but what does that have to do with Raphael and why is the woman carrying a fish?"

"Well, as it turns out, Sarah wasn't Tobias' only problem. His father had been stricken blind when he looked up to the sky and a bird pooped in his eyes."

"You're making this up, aren't you?"

"No. It's in the Book of Tobias."

"I'm not the biggest church-goer around, but I'm pretty sure there isn't any Book of Tobias."

"Not in the Protestant Bible, but it's in the Catholic and Eastern Orthodox Bibles. There are seven books in the Catholic Old Testament that aren't included in the Protestant. They are known as the Apocrypha."

He looked through the bookcase and produced an old Bible.

"I never thought of you as a religious type, Roger."

"I'm not, but I was raised in the loving arms of the Catholic Church," he said as he thumbed through the book. "See, here it is. The Book of Tobit, also known as the Book of Tobias."

"Okay, so Tobias' father is blinded by bird poop. What next?"

"Sarah's father is so happy to finally have her wed he gives half of everything he owns to Tobias. Tobias returns home from Medina with Sarah and Azariah in tow to tell his father the good news. Along the way, they stop at a stream and this huge fish lunges out at Tobias. Azariah tells him to grab it by the gills and drag it ashore. There, they slaughter it and Azariah tells Tobias to save the entrails and they will heal his father's eyes. When they get home, Tobias anoints his father's eyes with the fish entrails, just as Azariah said to, and his father's vision is restored. Well, they were so thankful they tried to give Azariah half of everything they owned."

"Sounds like a standard way of saying thanks," she said.

"They did things differently in those days. Anyway, they tried to give him half of everything they owned. But, to their amazement, Azariah refuses their gift and reveals himself to be the archangel Raphael, telling them to give thanks to the Lord, instead. It's a great story about the unforeseen. Tobias met Azariah and it changed the rest of his life, the lives of Sarah and her family, and even the life of Tobias' father. What if Tobias had blown off Azariah as a crazy old man and gone about his travels alone?"

Patricia nodded in understanding. "I get it. The young woman in the painting represents Raphael in disguise."

"Yes. And, Raphael is the patron saint of travelers, healing and lovers, among a bunch of other things."

"I'm guessing it's the lovers part you prefer."

"What can I say? I love women. Which is why I prefer Saint Raphaela to Saint Raphael."

"What would the Pope say if he knew you were changing the gender of the archangels?"

"He just might get a kick out of it."

"I guess that makes her your patron saint."

Patricia noticed how Roger looked at the painting with some sentiment and a little smile, but didn't answer.

Chapter Ten

"Jana? Could you come in here, please?"

Jana could see how stressed the older woman was.

"How bad is it?"

"Bad enough. I don't know how to get out of this mess. I need help. Is there anyone Roger did business with that might be able to give me advice? Someone that might know what Roger was thinking?"

Jana went to her desk and was gone several minutes before she returned.

"There's one guy, Neal Dent. But, I always thought there was something strange about him. Roger told me he's known Neal since childhood, but they never did business together. Roger was pretty particular about who he did business with. So, I always wondered, why wouldn't he do business with his oldest friend?"

"Why did Roger do anything? Why did he select me to manage his estate? Maybe there was never an opportunity for them to do business together. Who knows? But, if he was Roger's oldest friend, I need to talk to him. Do you have his contact information?"

Jana handed her the note she had been holding with his number.

But, as Patricia started dialing the number she couldn't help but wonder why she had never heard of Roger's closest friend before this moment.

§§§§§

"Mr. Dent? My name is Patricia Kennealy. I'm the executor for Roger Tucci's estate."

"Call me Neal. Thank you for taking care of him. He was a good friend."

"It was my pleasure. I was just following his wishes. And, that's why I'm calling. I understand you've known Roger a long time."

"We met in fifth grade and have been friends since."

"I'm sorry to bother you on a weekend, Neal. But, I was wondering if you could take the time to help me with some of Roger's business deals."

"Well, I'd be glad to help. Tell me what I can do."

131

Neal listened quietly while Patricia filled him in on the situation, letting her finish before saying, "I'll tell you what, I'll take a look and give you whatever advice I can. When can we get together?"

"I'm working on getting his affairs straightened out. I'll be here in his office all weekend."

"That's good. Give me an hour and I'll meet you there."

After she hung up, Patricia thought again about what Jana had said. Why didn't Roger ever do business with his oldest friend?

§§§§§

"Who was that?" his wife Jane asked after Neal got off the phone.

"Oh, just one of Roger's floozies. Roger put her in charge of his business affairs and now she can't handle it. She was calling for help."

"What are you going to do?"

"I'll help her out, of course. It's for Roger."

She smiled as she patted his hand. Neal smiled back.

§§§§§

He put down the documents he had been reading before turning to Patricia.

"The situation isn't good. Some of this stuff doesn't make sense. I don't really follow what he was thinking. Unfortunately, he signed contracts and put down deposits, so you're left to work with them best as you can. The way I understand it is you have a whole bunch of obligations and not enough money to cover them."

"Yeah, that's it in a nutshell. My only hope is if the conference is a big success. The big problem is it isn't anywhere close to being a success – big or small. Neal, I don't have a background in business. I don't know what Roger had in mind and I'm in over my head. I need some help."

"What you need to do is get rid of as much of this debt as you can."

132

"We don't have enough money to do that. We barely have enough to pay for the conference. And, Roger set it up so we can't get to the registration money until we can pay the accounts he signed."

"It would be nice to get hold of that money, but you don't need it. For instance, tell the people who own the auto loan to come and take the car. That will get rid of several thousand dollars in debt right there."

"But, the car is worth more than the amount he still owes. I was hoping to sell it and get a little cash."

"Not worth your time. Same thing with the apartment complex. Let them eat the loss."

Patricia nodded to indicate her understanding.

"But, what about his deposit?"

"Again, not worth your time. Apartment complexes almost always take the deposit anyway. You weren't going to see any of it. The next thing I would do is to call up the credit card companies and tell them Roger is defaulting. What are they going to do? Ruin his credit score? Besides, they've already factored in things like this. It's just part of doing business to them."

"And, what about Jana?"

"I'm sorry for the girl, but she must have known what she was getting into. Life is tough."

"Yes, I see what you mean. Everything you're saying is all very good advice and I'll give it some real thought."

"It sounds to me as though you have a choice. You can tell all of these other people tough luck, or you can pay the bills out of your own pocket. It's up to you."

"What about the conference?"

"Cancel the conference and keep the money. Let people sue Roger to get their money back."

"What if we got more people to sign up? Wouldn't it be better to hold the conference than to default?"

"Sure, but how are you going to do that?"

"I was hoping you could give me some help."

133

"You need to get the word out. Do some advertising and contact people in the business."

"Where do you advertise for a marijuana grower's conference?"

"I don't have any idea. Like I said, my recommendation is to fold the tents and take what you can."

"What if I get more people to register? Could you help me run it?"

"I can help you with that. I've done conferences before and know what to do."

"Roger didn't tell you anything about what his plans might have been?"

"Patricia, the truth is, Roger wasn't altogether there these last few months. There's no telling what he was thinking. If he had specific plans, he didn't share them with me. If he didn't share them with someone like you, I don't know who he would have."

"What do you mean?"

"Well, I just assumed you were sleeping with him."

"Don't assume. I wasn't sleeping with him and I never did. Please don't say that again."

"Sorry. I just thought every woman he knew was sleeping with him. I didn't mean to offend you. Anyway, those are my recommendations."

"Thanks, Neal. I'll be in touch."

After he left she called Jana in.

"Well, I answered one question. I know why Roger never did business with Neal Dent."

§§§§§

"What can I do to help?"

Patricia had returned home after meeting with Neal and was now trying to get some of the tension to leave her body and mind. The opportunity to relax with her husband and children went a long way to helping her out.

"Keep doing what you've been doing," she told John. "Keep the home fires burning."

She sighed at the feeling of being overwhelmed. Her list of chores went way up with Roger's death and she became the executor of his will. Now, she not only had to take care of his business, but she had to liquidate his estate. And, there was no life insurance to pay for things. It had become so overwhelming she had been forced to take a leave of absence from her job. The thought of the lost income only weighed even more on her mind.

She was able to get the creditors to agree to take the car back for what was owed on it and was able to work out some deals with the credit card companies to give her time. The office rent was paid through the end of the month making it a near priority to move out by then. But, the highest priority was to clear out the apartment. He was already two months behind and she didn't want to keep adding to that debt. The manager, Preston Pickert, had been very generous and helpful, but she didn't want to push it. She had to get everything out of the apartment. Family members promised to go by and remove everything they wanted by the end of the week. After that, Patricia was free to dispose of the rest any way she could.

Patricia checked in with Jana every day to see how she was doing and to bring her up to date.

"I need to stay here in Cisco for the rest of the week. I brought files home with me and I can work from here for the next few days. I'd like for you to get hold of everyone on Roger's call list and ask them to help pack. Tell them they are welcome to help themselves to a memento, as long as they help pack his things. Tell them to bring packing material, if they have any. We need to get everything out of the apartment before Monday. The family members only need to go by the office to get in. I'll have the apartment manager leave the apartment unlocked Saturday morning. People will be able to go in and get to work. Phone calls, text messages, emails, whatever works, just contact as many of his friends as you can. I'll be there as soon as I can. Do you think you'll have time for that?"

"Time is something I have plenty of. Things aren't exactly bustling around here anymore."

"Well, that's going to change as we get closer to the conference date. Let's get as much as possible in order while we have a chance."

135

"You're committed to doing the conference?"

"I can't see any alternative, despite what Neal said. The only hope we have is to make the conference a success. But first, we need to get out of the apartment."

Surely, she thought after she hung up, *this will work out well. What could go wrong? These are Roger's friends. They'll help. Yeah, right. Keep telling yourself that.*

It's a straight, two-hour shot from Cisco to Dallas' Greenland Hills where Roger had his apartment. With streets named McCommas, Morningside, Mercedes, Merrimack and Monticello, it was commonly referred to as the 'M' Street Area. Returning to the area where she and John had started out pleased her. She noted with nostalgia the apartment they had shared together as newlyweds and the house Roger had lived in when they had met. So much had changed. But, at the same time, so much was still the same.

Patricia noted the number of cars in the parking lot when she arrived, far more than she remembered seeing those times she stayed at the apartment, and hoped it meant a good turnout. But, instead of being encouraged, she had a feeling of foreboding as she approached the open door to the apartment and saw Jana was standing there, waiting. When she saw Patricia approaching she met her on the sidewalk.

"Before you go in, let me give you a little warning."

"The fact you were waiting is all the warning I needed. Thanks, Jana."

The scene that greeted her was reminiscent of a Friday night college frat party. It was only a little after 10 o'clock in the morning, but the party was in full swing with empty liquor bottles littering the room and ashtrays full of cigarette butts. People were laughing, drinking and talking. She could spot only a few boxes with hardly anything in them. No one greeted Patricia when she arrived.

Without comment, Patricia went back to her car and returned a few minutes later with a vacuum cleaner and a bucket of cleaning supplies. Dropping the bucket off in the kitchen, she plugged the vacuum cleaner in and began to vacuum. She began in the living room, making sure to intrude into conversations. Patricia saw Jana begin collecting glasses and ashtrays, not bothering to notice if they were still being used. But, then again, maybe she did.

Those there to work would stay and work. Those there to party would get annoyed and leave. Within ten minutes it was just the two women. Once they were alone,

Patricia stopped and said to Jana, "Now we know why Roger turned to me and not one of them."

With the crowd gone, Patricia was able to make a survey of what was left in the apartment. The family had removed many items, including Roger's library. The crowd had taken some loot with them. The remainder wasn't as bad as she feared, but now it was just the two of them when she had hoped for some real help. They couldn't do it all by themselves.

She sat and looked at the remains of what had once been Roger's beloved study. Dead less than a week and already any evidence of his existence was rapidly disappearing, she thought. It made her sad and she nearly started crying again. But then, she saw something wonderful hanging right in front of her – St. Raphaela. It amazed her that no one had claimed it. It wasn't a valuable painting, and that probably explained it, but it was a true memento of Roger.

She carefully removed the painting from the wall and wrapped it in a towel to protect it. On her way out to the car she said to Jana, "If you want to, be sure to take something to remind you of Roger. I have the only thing I want."

§§§§§

"Jana, there's no way we can do all of this ourselves. If we want to be out of here by Monday we're going to need some help."

"I know. I started calling some charities while waiting for you. I told them they could have everything if they would help us. The best I could get was they could help in a couple of weeks. They'll be glad to take it if we deliver it, but I couldn't find anyone who could help with the moving out."

Patricia let that sink in before responding. "That was good thinking. Thanks for trying. But, what do we do now? Any ideas?"

Jana paused before answering. "I know someone who might help. They do volunteer work with the Dallas Diocese. I met them there."

"Give them a call. If they can help, I sure would appreciate it."

"Alright. Give me a few minutes," she said and left the apartment. Patricia spent the time making a mental list of the things they would need to get done. The furniture would just go out, but the small items would need to be packed. She had promised the apartment manager the apartment would be clean and empty, so she and Jana would have a big cleaning job ahead of them. But if they could get everything out of the way, it should go pretty easily, she thought. She was just finishing her list when Jana returned smiling.

"Success! They'll be here in a few minutes," she said.

"Oh, thank you, Jana. That is such a relief." With one issue taken care of, Patricia got to work on the other issues and was busy loading boxes when a team of women arrived. Much to her relief, she saw they were dressed in faded jeans and work shirts. Unlike Roger's friends, they clearly came ready to work.

Introductions were made and everyone got busy. A couple of women had brought tool boxes with them and got busy taking all of the doors off. "We'll need the extra couple of inches to get things out," one of them told her. With quick efficiency, they went to work dismantling the furniture and moving the pieces out to waiting pick-up trucks and vans. "We've done this quite a bit," a middle-aged blonde explained. "The Diocese calls us all the time and we love helping them out. We have an understanding with them." Patricia thought this last comment somewhat curious.

The team of women tore through the apartment like a buzz saw. Patricia ordered pizza delivered for everyone and the women barely paused to eat. By the middle of the afternoon, the apartment was completely cleared out. Everyone was sweaty and tired as they put the final touches on their loads, but the team of women was still smiling and laughing as Patricia approached.

"I can't express how thankful I am. We would never have been able to do all of this on our own."

"Everything is being donated to Harbor Ministries Life Training Center and that should be plenty. They'll be able to do a lot of good with your donations. But, if you feel you need to make an extra contribution, you can make a donation to Saint Nicholas."

Patricia was a little confused but managed to say, "Sure. I'll be glad to."

With that, the women got in their vehicles and were gone.

Patricia and Jana finished cleaning the empty apartment and called Preston Pickart to inspect it. He barely looked around and said he was satisfied as Patricia handed him the keys.

"Where can we send the check for the deposit?" he asked.

"Check? I owe you forty-five hundred dollars," she said.

"I spoke with management and they were fine with everything. You've been honest and upfront with us and I'm authorized to tell you the Essex Apartments appreciates it. Roger Tucci was a good tenant. We appreciate his business and we're sorry to hear about his death. We wish you the best."

As they were leaving, Patricia told Jana about their helpers' comment about how she could make a contribution.

"I thought it was very strange. I wonder why she wanted me to make a contribution to Santa Claus," she said to Jana.

"Santa Claus?"

"Yeah, she said I could make a contribution to Saint Nicholas. Isn't that Santa Claus?"

"Yes, but he's also the patron saint of prostitutes."

Patricia stopped walking and turned to face her.

"What are you trying to tell me?"

"They were all prostitutes. They have a high-priced brothel in the Highland Park area. I understand their clientele includes some of the richest men in Texas. Some of the richest women, too."

Patricia silently stared at her. Jana asked, "Are you okay? Are you mad?"

Patricia finally started laughing, "No, I'm not mad. I was just thinking how appropriate that was. Roger would have loved it. Thank you, Jana."

"Are you kidding me? They were probably business associates of his."

Interlude

The papers had to be in the mail today or the deal would fall through, and he still needed Herman Lipton to sign the contract. Finding he had left his office for the day, Roger rushed over to the Lipton residence. Herman was there, waiting for him. They went into the living room where Roger produced the papers for Herman to sign.

"Here are the financials. You need to sign here that you've seen them." Roger watched as he signed before producing the next form, working through the pile one document at a time. As they were finishing, Herman's wife, Dena, came in and asked if she could fix them anything. Roger started to answer, "No, thanks, Dena, we're..." and stopped mid-sentence when he saw her face. She was holding one side away from him in an attempt to hide the black eye.

Herman realized Roger was staring at Dena and said, "It's no big deal, Roger. She had an accident. That's all."

Roger turned his gaze at Herman. Without a word, he picked up the documents and tore them in half, placing the torn documents in his briefcase.

"Roger! What are you doing? You can't do that! We have an agreement in place."

Roger didn't say a word as he picked up his briefcase and walked towards the door.

"Stop! Listen to me, this doesn't mean anything! I got carried away, that's all. I apologized and I'll make it up to her. It's no big deal. This is a family matter and isn't any of your business."

Roger looked at him with ice in his eyes and told him, "Everything my business partners do is my business. If this is how you treat your wife, what does that say about what you'll do to me? If you can't be trusted with your own wife, how in the world could I ever trust you with my money? Besides, I get to pick the people I do business with. I always had a bad feeling about you Herman. I couldn't quite put my finger on it before, but now I know why."

With that, he walked out the door.

Later, Kristen found Roger sitting in his study at home.

"Did you close the deal with Herman Lipton? You said you needed to get the papers mailed today."

Roger quietly shook his head. "There won't be any deal. I called it off."

"Oh, Roger. You said it was worth a lot of money."

He nodded as he answered, "Yes, it was."

"What happened?"

"I saw his wife. He had been beating her."

"And, you canceled the deal because of that? Are you mad?"

"I'm surprised. I thought you would be supportive. I thought you would agree that we can't do business with a wife beater."

"Listen to me, Roger. I don't appreciate what he did, but it isn't your business. Are you going to cancel every business deal when you find out the other side does something you don't approve of? You won't be able to find any partners at all if you do that. Besides, do you think you're so lily white you can afford to pass judgment on others? What about your philandering? Don't you think some people would object to that just as much as you object to someone beating their wives? I know I do."

"No, I'm no better than the next guy, I know that. But, character counts and when I have to make decisions about whom I do business with I have to consider everything. If he treats his wife that way, you can bet it's only a matter of time before he does something abusive towards me."

"But, all that money!"

"Is that the only thing you're worried about? The money? I've always taken pretty good care of you and we have money in the bank. So what if we don't have that contract? There will be others."

"But, we could've had more!"

She picked up a paper weight on his desk and threw it at him. It missed as he ducked, but he turned to her with wide eyes.

"What are you doing?"

"We're done, Roger," she yelled at him.

"We were done years ago. I've been hanging around for the sake of the children. I was warned about women like you, women who are cold in bed, but I ignored it. You were the only woman I ever fell in love with. But, I was told you would make my life miserable and you have."

The anger burned in her eyes as she said, "I want you out of this house. I want you out right now! I'm taking everything. I'm cleaning you out. The house, the cars, the bank accounts, everything! You seem to enjoy starting over from nothing. Well, you can do it again. Now, get out of here!"

Roger shrugged his shoulders and started to walk out when he suddenly stopped. Without saying a word, he took the painting of St. Raphaela off the wall and left with it under his arm.

Later, sitting in the bar of the hotel where he checked in, he thought of how he had failed in his role as husband. "You must lead safely", he had been told. "If you breach the trust by not acting responsibly and in the proper manner, you will be replaced.' He realized, that from Kristen's perspective, he had breached her trust by not acting responsibly. She wanted money, the more the better. He had known she was a gold-digger from the beginning, but married her anyway. He thought he could handle her, but had failed. Could he blame her for being what he always knew she was? He had not led safely and now, she had replaced him. It wasn't, he realized, all Kristen's fault. He had played his part in causing the marriage to fail.

There wasn't anything he could do about his own marriage and he didn't want to. The children were grown. He was grateful to Kristen for that. He loved his children and was glad he had always been a part of their lives. He didn't really think the news would be a surprise to them, though.

But, he thought he could do something positive about one situation while calling the police.

"I want to report an assault, please." He described what he had seen at the Lipton house to the dispatcher.

"Did you actually see the assault take place, sir?"

"No, she already had the black eye when I arrived."

"I'm afraid there isn't anything we can do, sir. Unless she wants to file charges, they can always claim the bruises came from something else."

"But, he admitted to me he hit her."

142

"Were there any other witnesses to that statement?"

"No, it was just us three."

"Then, they can deny he ever said it. I'm sorry, sir. Our hands are tied. Maybe the law will change some day, but as it stands now, unless she files charges or the assault is actually witnessed by someone, there is nothing we can do."

Roger realized getting angry with the dispatch wouldn't change anything and simply thanked him before hanging up. The next day, while Herman was at work, Roger went by and used his powers of persuasion on Dena to convince her to leave. Later that evening, he was at a restaurant when Herman showed up. Roger stood as Herman charged at him, hitting him full in the face and knocking him to the ground.

"You bastard! Where's my wife?"

"Somewhere you'll never find her," he said as he got back to his feet. Waiters had rushed up to restrain Herman and Roger knew he wouldn't be attacked again. Herman shook them off and started to leave.

"This isn't over, Roger! I'm coming after you."

Roger was thankful for those words, they sounded very nice in the police report when Roger filed assault and battery charges against Herman. The pictures of the bruise on his face was a nice touch. His demands to drop the charges included granting Dena a generous divorce settlement and never bothering her again.

When she showed up to thank him she said, "I don't understand how he was able to hit you like that, Roger. I know you boxed in college. I would think he would never have been able to land one on you."

Roger smiled. He didn't tell her how he had left instructions with his office to tell Herman where he could be found – in a restaurant with plenty of witnesses.

"Just lucky, I guess."

His own future was different, though. It didn't take long to finalize his divorce from Kristen and she was good to her word. She took everything he had. He didn't care and was wealthy again within a year. Meanwhile, Kristen burned through all of the money from the divorce and was broke before too long. When his children told him about her situation he set up a generous trust for her. It would give her a nice allowance so she could live comfortably for the rest of her life without giving her the ability to lose it all. She never thanked him for it.

"If they say I never loved her, you know they are a liar," he thought. "We chased our pleasures here and dug our treasures there. But, she had arms that changed and eyes that lie."

Chapter Eleven

"Patricia, I'm not comfortable having my father's memorial service in a church. We never went to church when we were kids and never really discussed religion. I don't even know what his views were about religion. I think having a memorial service there is inappropriate."

Patricia nodded her head, "I agree."

"Good. Then it's settled. I have some ideas for the service I would like to discuss with you."

"No."

"What, do you have your own ideas?"

"No, that isn't it. We're going forward with the plans as they are. I agree with you it's inappropriate, but those were your father's wishes. He was very specific and wrote out the details. Your father wanted a memorial service in a church and specifically asked for this church, Saint Thomas Aquinas, and specifically wanted Father Francis to preside. Quite frankly, I never thought the church would agree, but Father Francis didn't even hesitate when I approached him about it. He agreed to everything. The church won't hold a funeral mass on Sunday during the Easter season. That's why it's on Saturday."

"But, Patricia, you're the executor of his estate so you can do what you want."

"I am doing what I want. I want to follow his last wishes. That is why you put those kinds of things in writing."

"There's nothing I can do to change your mind?"

"Not unless you can get your father to tell me something different."

After Roger's son left Patricia reflected on how Roger's son said his father had never discussed religion and thought, *I wonder if he ever paused to consider how his father named him Jacob and his brother and sister are Joseph and Sarah.*

§§§§§

The church was full and as Father Francis looked out from the pulpit he was neither surprised nor disappointed to see that women made up a disproportionate number

145

of the people there. That, he knew, was one of Roger's special abilities. Neither was he surprised at the level of diversity. Here were people of all races, all faiths, all walks of life. Many had probably never been in a Catholic church before and likely never would again. The thing they had in common was that Roger had somehow touched their lives. Each of them was lost in his or her thoughts as the priest began the service.

"May the God of hope give you the fullness of peace, and may the Lord of life be always with you."

Using the printed ceremony, the congregation replied, "And also with you."

Oh, my god. How will I ever find another lover like Roger? That man sure knew his way around a woman's body. I'll never look at a purple shirt the same way again.

"The grace and peace of God our Father and the Lord Jesus Christ be with you."

"And also with you."

Oh, please. Don't let anyone look in the urn.

"The grace and peace of God our Father, who raised Jesus from the dead, be always with you."

"And also with you."

Don't worry, Roger. You taught me well. I'll be fine.

"May the Father of mercies, the God of all consolation, be with you."

"And also with you."

I should have shot the bastard for sleeping with my wife. She ended being a much better lover as a result and that's probably what saved the marriage. Still, ...

"We are gathered here today in this Vigil Service to give praise and thanks to God for Christ's victory over sin and death, to commend the deceased to God's tender mercy and compassion, and to seek strength in the proclamation of the Paschal Mystery. Lord, we ask for your blessing this day as we say farewell to Roger Virgil Tucci."

I barely knew him, but I'm rich today because I took a couple of minutes to listen to his business pitch all those years ago. I'm thankful I did.

"This is a time to remember Roger and to commend him to God. In prayer we ask God to console us in our grief and give us strength to support one another. Consoled by the redeeming word of God and, by the abiding presence of Christ and his Spirit, we call upon the Father of mercy to receive the deceased into the kingdom of light and peace."

A snow storm and dead body. I guess it's the things you're the least prepared for that change your life the most.

The ceremony continued with prayers and readings from the psalms and gospels, finishing with the singing of a chosen hymn.

"Those of you who knew Roger well are probably wondering why he chose to have a memorial service in a church. He was raised Catholic, but that isn't why we are here today. The reason is Roger promised me he would come to my mass someday. This is his way of keeping his promise."

Well, that explains a lot. With all of the women he slept with, I'm surprised the roof doesn't open up and lightning strike us all dead.

"I have known Roger for many years and he was the one who taught me how to be considerate of others and to pay attention to the way I treat the people around me. Those lessons were important in my decision to enter the clergy. If I was not presiding over this service, I would be sitting there with you, paying my respects to an old friend. It is a great honor for me today.

"Roger taught me how many people either 'tell' or 'ask' when they're communicating to others. Telling, he said, is the most widespread way. Most of us have been conditioned to understand that telling is what other people understand best. We say sit, stay, giddyap, whoa, roll over, come, heel, back up. This is the way most people train their animals; they tell them what to do and expect them to obey. Unfortunately, that is how too many people communicate to other people.

"When you do what you are told, you are rewarded. When you disobey, you are punished. Within this situation, there is no room for opinion, judgment, intuition, expression or instinct. You are merely performing a task because someone is telling you to do it. How do you feel when you are around someone who is always telling you what to do?"

"The problem with telling as communication is that the only two options given for performance are reward and punishment. The reward is not necessarily something you want, but rather something the teller wishes to give you. The negative support of punishment is nothing more than do this or you will suffer in some way. Have you ever

147

raised your hand in anger as if you were about to hit your dog? You may find that in the future just the raising of your hand will cause a shying away.

"More often than not, the reward for obedience is nothing more than not being punished. For example, you kick your horse to get him moving. If your horse begins to walk, the reward is that life goes on without reprimand. If your horse does not begin to walk, he gets kicked harder. In effect, the only reason your horse moves at all is to avoid being kicked more severely.

"These are things Roger taught me. These are lessons to take into our professional lives, and these are lessons to take into our personal lives. How do you treat your friends, your children, your spouse? Do you tell, or do you ask? I have kept these lessons in mind as I have served my congregation and have been thankful for them. And, I have been thankful for Roger's friendship.

"Roger's friend, Patricia Kennealy would now like to speak."

Patricia knew giving a eulogy would be difficult. She hoped she could get though her prepared remarks without falling apart.

"I'm privileged to have known Roger for many years. I learned a lot from him over that time span. I'm sure we all have heard him talk about the decision making process he would go through. 'Consider all options and throw out what you can't do. Usually, there're only a few things left.' This, he would tell you, makes it easy to decide.

"When I was writing this eulogy, I didn't know what to say. Where was I suppose to start and how was I to portray Roger to a group of his friends and family, many of whom knew him better and longer than I? So, I followed Roger's advice. I examined all the options and looked at what was left.

"I considered telling stories about his life. I thought about talking about his business dealings. I considered discussing the way he helped so many charities and people with his generosity. In the end, I rejected them all. That, to me, wouldn't tell the story of Roger Tucci.

"Above all, Roger was about people communicating to each other. This is something Roger excelled at. His ability to understand what you were saying, what you were thinking, was uncanny. It was almost as if he could read your mind. This is how he was able to be such a good business partner and friend. He could communicate like no one else I've ever met.

"Roger told me communication is a two-way process. Both people in a conversation are sending a message, but each person also needs to show they understand what they are hearing. Few people really hear what is being said to them. Roger always heard. And, he always saw what he was looking at. It was a special gift he had.

"In this way, he affected people far beyond what could be expected or predicted. And, this is another lesson he taught me. Our actions result in effects going far beyond what we could expect. There are people here today who never met Roger, or knew him for only a short while, but still had their lives changed by his actions.

"We had a number of conversations about it and I wish I could recall all of what he said, but it was mostly over my head. Frequently, it sounded somewhat mystical, but he assured me there was nothing strange about it. Roger used to tell me there is only one thing that stands between two people from performing in unison. Only one hurdle separates the perfect combination of two people in pursuit of a common goal. It is communication. People who can communicate successfully, he said, can do anything. Anything!

"I was frequently awed at the things that Roger would do. He would tell me things about someone simply by observing them. He would know their needs and thoughts by observing them, by seeing them, and he could understand what they wanted. He could tell me what someone was going to say, and he was nearly always right. They were communicating to him without even knowing it. In reality, we are all communicating like that. Roger was simply able to receive the message better than most of us.

"Great business people are great communicators. People already know how to do the things they're supposed to know at that level. If someone knows how to do something and you want him or her to do it, all you have to do is effectively communicate this. The person will do it if a healthy working relationship has been established. The same is true in personal relationships, and this is where Roger was at his best.

"When I think of Roger, these are the things I remember. I will remember him as someone who would listen to what you had to say and would show he understood what you said. I don't know if I've ever met anyone who did it better. It was a true gift. I don't know where he learned to do it, but I'm glad he did. I'm thankful for knowing him. I'm thankful for his gift. I'm thankful for the way he changed my life. And, I'm thankful to whomever it was who taught him these skills."

Patricia sat down, thankful she was able to keep control. Overwhelmed with emotion, she held John's hand and was only faintly aware as Father Francis ended the service.

"May almighty God bless you, the Father, and the Son, and the Holy Spirit."

"Amen."

I wonder if they're serving cocktails after the service.

The service proceeded to the graveyard next door. Traditionally, the Catholic Church did not support cremation. But, it had adapted to changing times and now allows it. It preferred for the cremation to be conducted after the vigil, but that was not possible in Roger's case. Still, it required the cremains to be buried.

Jacob, as the oldest child, was to carry the urn to the gravesite and walked to the urn after the service. Patricia watched with horror as he opened the urn and looked in. To her relief, he merely nodded his head very slightly and closed it again. After the crowd proceeded to the grave, Father Francis performed the burial service as the urn was placed in the ground and covered. Patricia cried on John's shoulder, barely aware of the sound of other women weeping around her.

With John in tow, Patricia approached Father Francis afterwards and said to him, "Thank you for the service, Father. I know Roger wasn't a member of your congregation. It was very generous of you."

"Roger and I were old friends. We were poker buddies. I was very pleased to do this for him."

"Poker? Really?"

"What? You think because I'm a priest I don't like to play games? We had regular games for years. He was the most amazing player I've ever seen. He could've gone pro, if he had wanted to."

"I can picture him taking everyone's money."

"No, just the opposite. He pretty much broke even every game. I don't think he ever made or lost more than a few bucks in a game. That can't happen by chance, not for the number of years I saw him play. He probably felt taking our money was so easy it would be like theft."

"Well, I guess that means you've been to his place..."

"Many times."

"...and you must have seen his St. Raphaela painting."

"Oh, yes. I'm not sure when he got it, but I know he had that painting for a long time. That and his books were the only household items he took when he split up with his wife."

"How do you feel about Roger turning the archangel into a woman?"

The priest shrugged his shoulders. "I don't see any harm in it. After all, who's to say the archangels are men in the first place? There's probably some story about it, but whatever it was, I'm sure Roger examined all of his options and rejected what didn't work."

Patricia gave a low chuckle. "I think we're all familiar with the process. I've always wondered where he got it."

"I suppose we'll never know now."

After the ceremony, Patricia was socializing with the attendees. An older woman, who spoke of knowing Roger for many years, asked her how she had met him.

"My husband and I had an apartment near his house and I needed to use a phone one day."

The woman paused in thought before exclaimed, "Oh, my god! You're that woman! I wasn't sure it was a true story!"

Patricia blushed as she acknowledged it really did happen.

She suddenly became aware of how the people around her simply stopped talking and the men were all looking in the same direction. When Patricia looked, she saw the crowd part to allow an incredibly beautiful woman pass through and approach her. As she got close, she held out her hand.

"Hello, Patricia," she said as they shook hands. "I'm Celeste Niven. I just wanted to thank you for the wonderful ceremony and the kind words you said about Roger."

Patricia couldn't help but stare at her, but composed herself enough to respond, "Thank you. He was a special man. It was a privilege to know him. Did you know him long?"

Celeste nodded her head, "Yes, we have known each other for several years. You might say I was a student of his."

"You were his lover, you mean. Quite frankly, there are a lot of women who fit that description."

"I was more than his lover. I was his protégé. Anyway, it was very pleasant to meet you. He told me wonderful things about you. Of course, he was right." She leaned in close to Patricia before saying, "And, don't worry about the urn. No one suspected a thing."

With that, she turned and left, leaving Patricia to wonder how she knew about the urn. She saw the way John watched Celeste as she walked out and went over to him.

"Let me guess, you think she's really sexy and would love to go to bed with her."

You couldn't blame John for being caught off guard, but he wasn't.

"Of course I want to go to bed with her. What, you think there's something wrong with me? Tell me the truth, would you want to be with a guy who didn't want to go to bed with her?"

"No, that would be pretty disappointing. She's an amazingly beautiful woman."

"Don't worry. I would love to have sex with her, but I would never make love to her. You're the only woman I want to make love to. And, just because my hormones tell me to go to bed with someone doesn't mean I will. I'm not going to do anything to hurt you."

"What if I didn't know?"

"I would know and that is enough."

He looked at her and smiled. "Have I told you lately how beautiful you are?"

"Yes, but you can do it again."

"You are wonderfully beautiful and I'm a very lucky man to have you in my life."

"You must have taken lessons from Roger."

"No, but I paid attention."

They were both quiet on the drive back to Cisco when Patricia broke the silence.

"I nearly had a heart attack when Jacob looked in the urn, but he was fine. Didn't you remove the ashes?"

"Sure. They're back home, waiting for you to decide where to spread 'em. I confess, I was surprised when he looked in there. But, when you think about it, people spread ashes all the time. I guess it's only natural for people to look."

"Then why wasn't Jacob upset?"

"Well, you don't think I was going to let you take an empty urn did you? What if someone looked in it? They would be expecting to see something. So I filled it with ashes from the fireplace. Even cleaned out the unburnt wood. No one will ever know."

"How does it feel to lie to the Catholic Church?" he asked after a few moments. "Father Francis was under the impression that was Roger in the urn."

"It's not the worst thing I've ever done. Besides, it was Roger's wishes. He wanted the show at the church, but he didn't want to be buried there. Mine's not to reason why…"

She continued after a short pause, "But, John, I was thinking about that woman, Celeste."

"This isn't going to be a problem, is it?"

"No, don't worry. I was just wondering, what was it about her that made her so beautiful? She has the same equipment other women have, so why did everyone see her as being so much more beautiful. And, let's be honest, the women noticed just as much as the men. Even I noticed."

John was silent for several seconds as he thought how to answer.

"It isn't about what you have, it's about what you do with it. We saw her as being beautiful because she knew she was beautiful. It's about knowing and being confident in your beauty. She radiated it. She absolutely knew she was beautiful and that meant no one would see her any other way."

"What about me?"

John gave a small laugh.

"What? You think that's funny?"

"No, not funny. Only unexpected. I'm sure you got some training from Roger at one time or another because you radiate beauty, too. I'm pretty sure I even know when it happened. But, whatever Roger said to you, I'm thankful."

Interlude

Roger got into the poker game circuit while at the University of Texas. The games were small stakes and he made sure never to win too much. It was so easy for him to read the other players he could have won big, if he wanted to. What he wanted was to socialize and make contacts, not clean out the other students.

It was during one of these games when a player dropped out and a big Hispanic guy took the seat across from Roger.

"Equi," he said when Roger introduced himself. He pronounced it '*eh-KWA.*'

"Your name is *here*?"

"That's *aqui*. I'm Equi. It's short for *Equivocado.*"

After his last comment, Roger hesitated before saying anything.

"I know what you're thinking. Yes, it means *mistake* or *misguided.*"

"Should I just let it go or is there a story here?"

"Yeah, there's a story. Before I was born, the doctor told my parents I was a girl. When the doctor in the delivery room told my mother she had just had a boy, she said he must be mistaken - *equivacado*. The nurse thought that was the name she was giving me. By the time anyone realized it, it was too late. Appropriately enough, it was a mistake."

"I'm sure you've heard every joke there is, so I'll leave it alone."

Equi smiled at Roger's comment. "Thanks. You're right, I have heard them all. The annoying thing is everyone thinks they're being some kind of original wit."

They saw each other frequently after that, eventually becoming good friends. As a result, Roger was one of the first to hear Equi was thinking of dropping out of school without finishing his degree.

"Equi, why would you invest three years and then quit? It doesn't make sense."

"No, it makes sense for me. I'm not interested in doing this. I'm wasting my time and my parent's money."

"This is crazy! What are going to do? How will you make a living?"

"Roger, I sat down and went through all of my options and this is the best decision."

"I'm not convinced. What do you mean you went through all of your options?"

155

"It's something I learned from my father. Whenever I was troubled about something, he would sit me down and we would look at all of my options. We would write everything on a piece of paper and examine every one of them. That's what I've been doing."

"The Sherlock Holmes act?"

"Sherlock Holmes? What are you talking about?"

"In the stories, Holmes would say, 'Once you eliminate the impossible, whatever remains, no matter how improbable, must be the truth.' That's what you're doing. Listing your options and eliminating the ones that don't work."

"I never thought of it that way, but yeah, that's what I'm doing. Basically, once you get rid of the ones you can't do, there's only a few options left. The decision-making gets a lot easier after that."

Equi continued, "So, I went through my options and nothing about staying in school worked out. The only option left was to leave school. I don't know what I'll do, but I know I won't find it here. I talked it over with my parents and they want me to come home for a while."

Roger was disappointed to learn his friend was leaving, but he understood they were destined to go their separate ways after graduation. This simply moved the date up.

"Well, listen. I know some girls in Dripping Springs. It's about 25 miles from here. What do you say we go out there for a couple of days before you leave? My treat."

Equi slowly nodded his head. "That sounds good. Let me throw some things together real quick."

Soon, the two men were in Roger's car, heading west out of the city. Austin in the early-1970s was still a small town, and it didn't take long to reach the edge of the developed areas. The highway to Dripping Springs was a small country road and the storm hit them while they were still driving. The sky turned a deep blue as the front suddenly blew in and it got so dark the streetlights came on. They could see the rain moving across the hills towards them. The violence of the storm hitting them made the car shake and the flood gates of rain opened on the two travelers.

The wind was blowing with near hurricane strength and, within seconds, the rain was so heavy Roger could barely see the road. Fearing for their safety, he looked for a safe place to pull over when he spotted a street to the left and quickly turned in to get off the highway. He let out a sigh of relief as he directed the car to the side of the road and came to a stop.

"We'll just wait here until it lets up," he said to Equi. He leaned against the steering wheel as he let his nerves calm down. He could swear it felt as though they were still moving. Suddenly realizing they really were moving, he sat up and looked around as Equi came to the same conclusion.

"Roger! We're moving! The water is sweeping us away!"

The road he had pulled into was a natural drainage and runoff from the main road was rushing down it. Thinking he was getting them to safety he had instead put them directly in harm's way.

"I can't steer. We're floating. We need to get out of here."

Roger started to open the door with the thought of jumping out before Equi grabbed his arm.

"Stop! If you go in that water you won't stand a chance."

"We can't stay here, either. If the car floods, we'll drown."

The rushing water caused the car to start turning. The vehicle was spun around and tossed without mercy for the two men trapped inside. The rain and rushing water was making it impossible to see. Roger rolled his window down and tried to look through the driving rain. What he saw froze his blood. They were headed straight for a low-water crossing with a brown raging flood of water and debris flying over the submerged road. It would be certain death for both of them if they were swept away.

"We have to get out of here now!"

Just as Roger said this they felt the car bump into something and momentarily come a halt, facing up the hill with water rushing over the hood and up the windshield, pouring in through Roger's open window. Equi's side of the car was closest to high ground and he forced his door open against the current.

"Jump! Now!" screamed Roger.

Equi pushed on the door and jumped into the raging water. Roger slid across the seat and was right behind him. Equi landed in knee-deep water and fought to stay on his feet in the current. The loss of his weight was enough for the car to float again and it started drifting down stream as Roger was jumping out, causing him to lose his footing. Equi had turned to help and saw Roger go down in the flood. Jumping into the water he grabbed Roger's leg as he was going under and held on as hard as he could. He knew if he lost his grip he would never find Roger again.

Roger fought to get up but one foot was caught in debris and the current pushed him down. He could feel Equi grabbing at him, trying to help him up, but the current was too strong. The flowing water was like a fire hose in his face, forcing water up his nose and into his mouth. He put one hand over his face to keep the water out as he fought to get his foot free. The pressure of the water was so great he couldn't fight against it and he was unable reach his foot to get free. Try as he could, he was helpless in the power of the flow bearing down on him.

The burning in his lungs told him he was running out of air. He had gone from safety to drowning in only a few seconds. He couldn't help but think that was the way life was. He never thought he would end up drowning in a flooded street. If they had just stayed home instead of going out this wouldn't have happened.

The burning was being replaced with a euphoric feeling of well-being and he relaxed with the knowledge the end was near. As he started fading into darkness he thought of how he ended up here, about to die. He only wanted a weekend with some girls and his love of women was about to kill him.

He was barely conscious when he felt his foot come free and he was lifted up into the air. Coughing and spitting up muddy water, he was only faintly aware of how someone was carrying him through the raging water. As he was dropped on the muddy ground he regained his senses enough to see it was Equi who had saved his life.

The rain was still coming down hard, but they were out of the flood waters. Gasping for air, he reached a hand over and squeezed his friend's arm.

"Thanks," was all he could manage to say.

The car was swept away by the flash flood and was eventually found nearly a mile downstream. The highway patrol took them to the local headquarters to make a report. The medical staff examined Roger and told him to get some rest, but he would be fine. It was a close call, but there was no serious injury. They were both seriously shaken up by the experience and the thought of a weekend away was out of the question. They had some friends come and take them back home.

It was nearly two weeks before Roger heard from his friend again. When he did, Equi asked him to come over to talk about something.

"You sound very serious," Roger said as he listened to his friend.

"No, not serious. Just very calm. I know what I want to do, Roger. You were a big part of the decision so I want to share it with you. Come over and we'll discuss it."

Borrowing a car, Roger was able to get over quickly, feeling ominous about what his friend had decided to do. When he arrived at Equi's apartment, Equi invited him in and asked him to sit down.

"Roger, something happened to me when we were in that storm. Something amazing. It's changed my life. I wanted to tell you about it. Roger, when I was out there, trying to pull you out of the water, I didn't have the strength. I tried as hard as I could, but I couldn't do it. The current was too strong. Your foot was trapped under a big branch and I couldn't get you free. I tried to lift if off you, but I couldn't even budge it."

Roger waited while his friend paused.

"I didn't have the strength to save you, so I asked God to help me. I prayed to him to give me the strength and He did. I called out to Him. I looked up into the sky and begged him to help me save you. And, He did. I was able to lift the branch with one hand and pick you up. Roger, I could feel Him with me. It was His strength, not mine, that allowed me to pull you out and get us both to safety. I couldn't do it by myself. I needed His help and He was there. He was there for both of us."

"Okay, God was there. Why are you telling me this? I can see you've made a decision. What are you going to do?"

"I'm joining the seminary."

Again, Roger waited. Equivocado was silent for several long seconds before continuing.

"I feel the calling. I want to serve God. I want to devote my life to the church. I've decided to go to the seminary. I want to be ordained. I have been discussing this with my church leaders and they're supporting me. They think I'm a good candidate."

"Are you sure about this? It's a big step."

"I've thought long and hard. You go around collecting lovers like butterflies. But, for me, illusions of that grand first prize are wearing thin. Yeah, I'm sure."

"How can you be so sure?"

"Remember how we talked about making a decision? List all your options. That's what I did. Everything was included, no matter how unrealistic. Then, I went through the list and looked at each one of them and drew a line through the ones that I couldn't do. I examined each and every one of them and thought hard about them. Some were easy to mark off, others were tougher. In the end, there was only one option remaining. The decision was easy after that. Believe me, I'm not doing this lightly."

"Why don't you let it sit for a while. Maybe you'll feel differently in a few days."

"I have no choice but to wait. You don't just knock on the seminary door and go in. There's a process. I'll have plenty of time to think about it, but I already know I won't change my mind. God called to me and I'm answering."

The two of them sat for a while without speaking. Finally, Roger asked him, "What name will you use? Father Equivocado won't inspire a lot of confidence."

"I already thought of that. I'll use my middle name. Francis."

"Father Francis. That'll work."

"Will I see you at mass?"

"Sorry, padre. It's not going to happen."

"Why not? I know you were raised Catholic."

"And, it was too dark. I spent my childhood listening to sermons about how we are all horrible sinners. According to the priest, I was going to hell. It was what they told people. I was human, therefore I was a sinner and I was going to hell. It haunted my dreams at night and turned me off to the whole church thing. After a while, I decided I needed to go my own way and I found a religious philosophy I'm comfortable with."

"What about any children you might have?"

"It's not up to me to decide how they worship, or even if they want to worship. They'll have to find their own way, too. But, don't worry. I'll stay in touch. And, I'll make you a promise. Once you get a congregation I'll attend one of your masses."

"Isn't it strange?"

"What?"

"The unintended consequences of our actions. We were on our way to meet up with some girls. Instead, you nearly drowned and I met up with God."

Roger nodded his head in agreement, remembering his thoughts as he was about to drown.

"Yeah, I've had similar thoughts lately. I wonder where this road is leading us."

Chapter Twelve

Patricia looked over her to-do list. She should have felt a sense of satisfaction for all of the tasks she had completed, but she didn't. She felt overwhelmed instead. She had never seriously considered Neal's advice about canceling the conference after she had learned the details. It wasn't the way Roger did business and she wasn't going to betray him. But, now she was stuck with managing the conference and she didn't even know where to start. Roger's initial efforts were either incomplete or so confusing Patricia and Jana couldn't figure out what he had in mind. Patricia suspected the cancer and pain killers had left Roger in a state he didn't fully know what he was doing.

A few more people registered for the conference, but not enough. As the number of people went up, so did the costs. More people meant a bigger, more expensive food bar. On top of the conference costs, they needed to make a profit to cover the rest of Roger's debts. Patricia did the math and figured they needed around 95 people to pay off everything – call it an even 100 to make sure. They were now up to a little over 40 and she couldn't see how they would be able to break even on the conference. Paying off Roger's debt was a pipe dream.

The problem was with getting the word out. They didn't have money to place ads but had written some press releases with the objective of getting free marketing in the news media. It had resulted in a few stories in the papers, but most media outlets didn't think it was significant enough to give it any coverage at all. The two women had been forced to rely on calling specific groups and people. Unfortunately, their contact list was small. Who do you call to invite to a conference about growing marijuana? Obviously Roger had thought there was enough of a market, but Patricia couldn't figure out how he planned on advertising and he hadn't left any notes about it. He had experience and resources she couldn't even begin to fathom. She had to find her own way to get the word out on a nation-wide basis. And, time was running out. The conference was only a few weeks away. Patricia was rapidly approaching the point where she would have to decide about following Neal's advice. The clock, she knew, was most definitely ticking.

They succeeded in getting the message to one group, though. The anti-marijuana groups had taken notice and had mobilized to block her progress at every opportunity.

Marijuana, they claimed, was the worst evil of today's modern society. To them, Patricia, by extension, was a demon in a dress. They had gone as far as calling the police in an attempt to have her arrested and had put pressure on the media not to run stories on her. The answer, she realized, was to make them work for her.

"Jana, do we have the contact information for the anti-pot groups?"

"Yes, it was all included in that complaint they made to the police. I have the address for the Baptist Coalition right here. Why?"

"I think I want them to accidentally get a memo."

§§§§§

"We are incensed that this woman would even consider doing something like this! First, she brings this illegal conference here to Dallas to promote growing an illegal drug and now she says she's going to lobby for a bill to decriminalize marijuana in Texas. This is just too much and we are here to protest this illegal action and this horrible woman. It isn't enough to put Dallas at risk, now she wants to put the entire state of Texas at risk. If it were up to her, this great state would be overrun with drug dealers and cartels."

Patricia watched the protesters in front of Roger's office with a little concern. Jana was standing next to her and said, "It's real mess out there."

"No, it isn't big enough. It's great the news is out there covering it, but there's only one local TV crew. We need more coverage. Do you think I could get them to throw things at my truck when I drive by? That would make some good news footage."

"Are you serious?"

"You bet. These people are doing everything they can to stop us. I think it's only appropriate they help us get the word out. But, this won't do it. I thought the leaked memo would get things going, but we need more."

"What do you have in mind?" Jana asked uneasily. She had helped Patricia draft the memo and had arranged for a friend to 'leak' it to the groups with the hope of inciting protests. So far, things had gone well and she was surprised Patricia wasn't satisfied.

164

"Do you think I could get them to attack me with the TV crew filming? I mean if I went down there and started an argument, do you think they'd attack me in front of the cameras?"

"Patricia! Stop that! You'd get plenty of press coverage – when they beat you to death. What would that achieve?"

She realized Jana was right and let it go. She was only half considering it anyway.

"Well, we need to do something to increase the news coverage. We haven't gotten a single new person to register in over a week. The conference is coming fast and we're running out of time," she said as she stood there with arms crossed.

It was then that good fortune struck in the form of a man walking in the door. Dressed in dress slacks, a long-sleeve white shirt and a tie, he looked at the two women and said, "I'm looking for Patricia Kennealy."

With suspicion, Patricia identified herself. The man held out his hand and said, "I'm pleased to meet you, Mrs. Kennealy. My name is Darius Hagerty. I'm with the Baptist Coalition. May we talk?"

Patricia was afraid she was about to get her wish to be attacked, but invited him into the inner office, asking Jana to come along. She wasn't sure if she was going to need a witness, but she felt reassured to have the young woman included.

"This is my assistant, Jana Genova. Please take a seat. What can we do for you Mr. Hagerty?"

"I have a business proposition for you."

Patricia looked confused.

"You need press coverage. So do we. I think we can work this thing to our mutual benefit."

Patricia took a quick glance at Jana before responding. "What did you have in mind?"

"That little protest out there is nice, but it won't amount to much in the way of advertisement. You've probably figured that out already." He noted her small nod before continuing. "We need to make a big splash for the press, something even the national media will cover."

Neither woman could figure out where this was going.

"I don't follow you, Mr. Hagerty. Are you saying you want to help us get publicity?"

"Absolutely! I know what you're doing. I saw right through that 'leaked' press release. You just wanted us to come out and protest and get on the news. The problem is a simple protest isn't news worthy anymore. Viewers have become too jaded. We need something bigger."

Patricia was wary but said, "I'm listening."

"What we need to do is provide the audience with a show."

"By 'audience' I'm assuming you mean the public."

"No. I mean the media. There is no way either of us can target a particular part of the public. We need to get the media to broadcast our messages to everyone. That's the only way we can get to the people we want to reach."

"Okay. So, what do you mean by a 'show'?"

"Controversy. The public isn't interested in talking heads discussing the news. They want action. They want to be entertained."

"I never thought of the evening news as being entertainment."

"It's a different world than the one our parents grew up in. People don't want to watch Walter Cronkite tell them the way things are."

"I'm not sure I see where you're going with this."

Hagerty leaned forward in his seat before answering.

"We stage a bunch of 'events' the news media can't help but cover. We have some fights and nasty arguments. The nastier, the better. They'll eat it up. Remember, they're fighting for ratings. If something comes along, they'll show it. It is pretty much what you're trying to do out there." He pointed out the window as he spoke. "We just need to spice it up."

Patricia was intrigued, but still not completely sold. "I wouldn't even know where to begin."

Hagerty handed her a folder he had been carrying.

"These are talking points. They'll give us a starting point. I'm providing you with the questions, claims and accusations I'll use. I had a team do some research and put together the most sensational ones. As you can see, they are quite inflammatory and are

166

certain to get some press coverage. They'll want to make sure they are providing equal time to both sides, so they'll contact you for a rebuttal. I've provided you with some material to help you in that regard."

Patricia briefly looked at the material he provided.

"Are you crazy? I'm not going to let you say these things."

"Well, you can't stop me from saying them. The only thing you can do is refuse to play along and that's your right. But, that won't help either of us. The more you play, the bigger the show will be and the more you'll get your message out. If they get some sound bites they'll put it on the news. All we have to do is put on some theatrics."

"Mr. Hagerty, I'll be honest with you. We don't have a 'message.' I'm not going to support any bill and I'm not interested in promoting marijuana."

"Then, why the conference? Why did you work to get the protest?"

"The conference was the brainstorm of a friend. When he died, I was left in charge. Now, there are thousands of dollars of debt I have to find a way to pay off. Going through with the conference seemed like the best idea. The problem is we can't get the word out to attract enough registrants. Right now, the conference isn't even paying for itself. I was hoping the demonstration would generate enough publicity to provide the advertising we need."

"Well, that's perfect. Every time you're mentioned on TV or the papers, they will have to mention your conference. The word will get out all over the country. You're bound to generate some interest."

"What's in this for you?"

"The same thing you get – publicity. Our donations go through the roof every time we do something like this. While I'm opposed to marijuana, I'm not very motivated to fight it. I think there are bigger issues out there we need to deal with. It doesn't bother me to help you out. If we put your conference in the news, my organization gets publicity at the same time and our contributions go up. We can use those contributions to fight for issues we do believe are important. We both benefit from this."

Patricia thought about what he had said, before shaking her head.

"No, I can't do this. I'm not trained or experienced at public debate. I'd look like a fool and then I wouldn't get anyone to register. There's too much to lose."

167

"I thought of that, too. I have an old friend, Milda Jinks, who will coach you on how to conduct yourself in front of the media. There isn't anyone better. By the time she gets done, you'll act like a polished politician. Remember, this doesn't work unless we put on a good show."

"You want us to put on an act. What's going to happen when the reporters figure that out?"

"Reporters might be skuzzy, but they aren't nearly as dumb as we like to think they are. They know what's going on and they'll play along. Their jobs depend on their ratings. If we give them what they need, they'll give us what we need."

She opened the folder and looked at the talking points again.

"You really think this will work?"

"I know it will work. I've done it before."

"You mean this goes on all the time?"

Hagerty simply smiled and sang, "*Money makes the world go 'round, the world go 'round, the world go 'round.*"

"You're going to make me cynical."

"Don't be. It's just a business like anything else. The public gets what the public wants. The media gets what it wants. We get what we want. Everyone's happy. That's all."

Patricia looked at Jana, "You've been awfully quiet. What do you think?"

"I think you don't have the money for my back pay yet and I don't think you will with the way things are going. You know the routine – consider your options…"

"If I hear one more person say that, I think I'll scream."

If she went along with his plan she would be at his mercy. This could all be a setup and she would be helpless if he betrayed her. She looked at Hagerty. What struck her about him was how he had smile lines in his face instead of frown ones. This wasn't a mean-spirited person. Jana was right – consider your options…

"Very well, we're in."

"Well, then. There's no time like the present to get started. We have a TV camera crew right outside. Walk out with me and play along. Get into an argument with me in front of the cameras. The nastier, the better. We'll have to ad lib this one."

168

Patricia was visibly nervous at the idea of what might happen.

"I don't think I can do that."

"Don't worry, I'm a big boy. I can take it."

"No, I mean, I'm so nervous I can't get angry about anything right now. I wasn't expecting to start right away. You said someone would come and coach me first." She was feeling weak by the time they reached the front door. Hagerty realized this proper housewife act wouldn't get the job done.

"This won't work. You don't look the part." He quickly stuck his hands in her hair and mussed it up. Before she could recover he asked, "Tell me something. When you give your husband a blow job, do you spit or swallow?"

Patricia's nervousness disappeared as her anger mounted and she felt the blood rushing to her face. But before she could speak, Hagerty loudly slammed the door open and headed towards the protesters. The TV crew swung their cameras his way when they heard the doors bang. Without slowing down, he shouted over his shoulder, "I tried to be reasonable, Mrs. Kennealy. Now, you'll have to deal with the entire weight of the Baptist Coalition! We have supporters all over this country and when we tell them what you're doing, you'll be hearing from them." Patricia was following hard and fast and the look in her eyes convinced him this was going to be good. The flushed face and tousled hair gave her just enough of a wild woman look.

The station ran – and reran – their exclusive on the events in front of Roger's office. The media department told the managers the clash between Hagerty and Patricia was pure gold. People either loved the way Patricia ripped into Hagerty or they hated it. Either way, they were watching it. The video quickly went viral and Patricia became an Internet sensation. She was soon swamped with calls for interviews. At the same time, donations poured in for the Baptist Coalition.

At home, John chuckled to himself as he watched the video again.

"Yep," he thought. "That's my red-headed fireball."

§§§§§

Few people would ever call the middleaged, over weight black woman attractive. But no one who knew Milda Jinks would ever call her stupid. At least, not more than once. Known for her coaching skills, she had become the quiet, backstage resource big name people relied on to make them look and sound like big name people when they spoke in public.

Darius Hagerty was waiting in the diner when she arrived. She purchased a cup of coffee and a croissant at the counter before joining him.

"Hi, Milda. How're you doing?"

"Good, Darius. Thanks for asking. I met with your girl."

"Did you give her my apology?"

Milda nodded. "Yes, and she said she understood what you were doing. She also said if you ever say something like that to her again she'll cut your dick off and make you eat it. I believe her, too."

"It gives a whole new meaning to 'spit or swallow,' doesn't it?"

"Well, it's nice you can maintain a sense of humor."

"Look, I'm sorry about what I said, but I knew she would never hold up in front of the crowd. I needed her to look convincing. It worked, too."

"Next time, leave the coaching to me, will you?"

"Sure. But tell me, what did you think?"

"She's pretty. The cameras will love her, especially that red hair. And smart, too. She'll be able to hold her own. But, she's raw."

"Can you coach her up to do the job?"

"Darius, I'm tempted to reach across this table and slap you. When have you known me to not be able to coach someone? Of course I can get her ready."

"Sorry, that's not what I meant. Let me rephrase my question. Can you coach her up quickly enough to be convincing? We don't have much time. We're already getting requests for interviews. If we don't act fast, this thing will die a natural death and we'll both be out of luck."

"How much time do we have?"

"Tomorrow."

Milda gave him a scathing look and got up from the table.

170

"Where are you going?"

"To get busy coaching Mrs. Kennealy."

§§§§§

The TV station covered the next confrontation between them and it was as exciting as cold oatmeal. Darius had coordinated with Patricia to have another run-in. The protesters were loud and garnered a lot of attention, but Patricia's reaction was unmoving. Milda met with Patricia in private after it was over.

"This may be business, but that doesn't mean we can't have some fun while we're at it. Spice it up. People are tuning in for a show. We want to make sure they get one."

"I thought people were tuning in for the news."

"Oh, no! They can get that anywhere. When they watch a show like this they want to see fireworks."

"I'm becoming increasingly disillusioned about our news media."

"Honey, you ain't seen nothing yet. It's much worse than you think."

"I don't think I want to know."

"Listen, you were milquetoast out there. A limp washrag. Understand what I'm saying?"

"Yeah, I get it. Spice it up."

"You need to put some fire into your statements. You sounded like you were repeating things from memory."

"I was."

"Well, it's commendable you learned your lines. But, there's more to it than that. Anyone can memorize lines. Not everyone gets to appear on the big stage. If you don't do better, you won't either. Stop thinking of this as an issue and think of it as a play. You're just one of the characters and you have a part to play. If you don't do your part, the whole show fails. What you need to do is think of something that will get you fired up."

"Swallow or spit?"

"I wasn't going to say that, but Darius knew what he was doing. Find some memory or issue that gets your blood pressure up. Think about it before the next confrontation and keep it handy in case you start to lose the passion."

"Like what?"

"Only you know that. Maybe it's some political position, or something you overheard at the coffee shop. Maybe a memory from your childhood. I don't know what it is, but it needs to be something that will make you want to rip Darius' face off. That's what everyone wants to see. If all they wanted was the facts, they would be reading *The New York Times*, not tuning into your show."

"Okay. I understand. I'll work on it. And, Milda? Thanks for your help."

"Don't worry about it. I'm glad to help. Besides, I love taking Darius' money."

§§§§§

The news coverage of his conflicts with Patricia energized the Baptist Coalition members and donations had poured in. Working quickly to take advantage of the energy, the Coalition put together a gathering with a large stage and a series of speakers. Darius Hagerty took the stage to loud cheers from his supporters.

"Can you believe, right here in Dallas, we have someone actively working to destroy society? Patricia Kennealy is doing nothing more than bringing drug pushers together in order to strategize a better way to break the law," he said to the adoring crowd.

"This is nothing less than organized crime! If Mrs. Kennealy has her way, the streets of Texas will be filled with drug addicts similar to the streets of Denver." The crowd roared its displeasure. "A friend of mine recently visited Denver and she told me how she was absolutely disgusted by the smell of marijuana the whole time she was in Denver. She also said that Boulder, Colorado has the same problem. She told me of how people were panhandling to get money and when they did, they would go to the nearest 'pot store' to get high. She also said that her relatives whom she was visiting were disgusted and had put up their house for sale because marijuana was a dangerous gateway drug. They reported to her that many marijuana users had graduated to cocaine or heroin;

172

hence, crime was on the increase. Insurance premiums also increased because of the probability that marijuana users would operate vehicles either during or after smoking the drug. Do we want that in Texas?"

The crowd roared their response. From where he was standing, Darius estimated there were nearly 5,000 people at the event. This was surely to make the news. Now, he only needed Patricia to show up and do her part.

"Are we going to stop it?" he asked them.

Again, the crowd roared their response.

"A study published in the Journal of the American Medical Association found the proportion of adults using and abusing the substance at least doubled between 2001 and 2013. So don't try to convince me that marijuana is a safe drug and don't try to maintain that marijuana sales will boost a state's income. Is the increased income really good when the cost to human lives is this bad? This is what Mrs. Kennealy wants to bring to Texas."

Suddenly, the crowd went silent with the shock of what they saw. There, right before them, was the very devil they were protesting against. They couldn't believe her brazenness at crashing their protest party. Darius, confused by the sudden silence, looked around and saw Patricia walking onto the stage. Approaching him, he put his hands up to protect himself as she grabbed the microphone from him.

"I've listened to this pompous ass tell lies about me and I'm here to defend myself. You might not want to believe what I'm going to tell you, but you won't be able to say you didn't at least hear it."

The crowd was so amazed they didn't know what to do. Patricia continued.

"My conference is not about breaking the law, it's about supporting it. We all have some law we object to. That doesn't mean people who support those laws are demons. I expect Mr. Hagerty to come to you with facts, not fairy tales. Who is this fabled person he's talking about? He quotes her, but how do we know what he says even happened?"

Some people recovered and began shouting at her to leave the stage, but she wasn't about to. Shouting to be heard over the protests, she continued.

"The fact is, medical marijuana helps with Alzheimer's, autism, cancer, seizures, PTSD and chronic pain. It has helped many Americans, including many veterans, stop using alcohol and hard drugs, both legal and illegal ones. Every minute an American dies of cancer. Every 19 minutes an American dies of a prescription drug overdose. Many vets become addicted to prescription opiates and die from them. Nobody has ever died from smoking too much pot. It is immoral to make marijuana illegal for anyone for even a second longer! For cancer patients, it's a matter of life and death."

By now the crowd was jeering everything she said in an attempt to drown her out. They didn't come here to have a balanced debate. They wanted to vilify the people they objected to and, at that particular moment, Patricia was number one on their list. She knew her part, though, and continued.

"Here are some more facts for Mr. Hagerty: over 16,000 jobs have been created since legalization. In states with legal marijuana, all crime is down. Murders in Denver alone in 2014 were down more than 50%. Teen drug use is down, traffic fatalities and suicides are down, alcohol consumption is down. What is there to not like about those statistics? And, don't forget the $70 million in tax revenue and $700 million in sales that stayed in the US and didn't go to the illegal cartels. Interestingly, three-quarters of all the legal marijuana users no longer use or buy prescription drugs."

While Patricia was talking Darius was able to get a second microphone and interrupted her at this point.

"Mrs. Kennealy must be sampling the goods because her numbers aren't right. $70 million is what was projected before the sales began, the number used to help sell the idea to voters. Colorado state officials have now confirmed the actual figure was only $44 million. But, they went out and made commitments greater than that. Now, they have to raise taxes to make up the difference. George Harrison was right:

If you drive a car, I'll tax the street.

If you try to sit, I'll tax your seat.

If you get too cold, I'll tax the heat.

If you take a walk, I'll tax your feet."

The crowd loved it and started singing the Beatles song.

"And notice how she doesn't address the effect it has on people's minds. A Northwestern University study found that marijuana users have abnormal brain structure and poor memory, and that chronic marijuana abuse may lead to brain changes resembling schizophrenia. The study also reported that the younger the person starts using marijuana, the worse the effects become. The American Medical Association argued against legalization and issued a report that said, 'Heavy cannabis use in adolescence causes persistent impairments in brain performance and IQ, and use is associated with increased rates of anxiety, mood and psychotic thought disorders.'"

Patricia jumped in and countered his argument.

"I have to wonder if Mr. Hagerty would still be so strongly against legalization if he bothered to get his facts straight. There is no evidence for long-term damaging effects in adults. Preliminary data linking marijuana use to an increased risk of schizophrenia have not been supported by further studies. The only confirmed long-term effect of marijuana use by adults is chronic bronchitis. And, keep in mind, it is still against the law to sell to anyone under the age of 18."

"Boy, look at how successful that has been with cigarettes!" The crowd roared their approval. "Do you think Mrs. Kennealy would be so supportive of marijuana if her own children started using it? Tell us, madam, do you use marijuana yourself?"

The crowd was getting into the debate, cheering Darius with every comment while trying to drown out Patricia's responses with yells and insults. But, Patricia had been well-coached and didn't let the crowd intimidate her.

"My personal habits have no bearing on this debate, one way or the other. I'm surprised you would stoop so low. Instead of trying to intrude in my personal life, why don't you discuss jobs? Legalization means jobs. There are the shops selling legal marijuana instead of the street dealers working for the cartels. There are jobs for the farmers here in the US, instead of supporting pot growers in other countries. And there are jobs for scientists to analyze products for purity and safety and develop new strains. These are all good, solid jobs paying income taxes and not paying the drug cartels. Our conference is bringing together high-tech people and investors for the purpose of creating jobs. Why is Mr. Hagerty so opposed to putting Americans to work?"

"What a great way to make a living! By preying on the young and innocent."

"There's nothing young and innocent about the Marijuana Growers Conference. These are scientists and business people looking for investment opportunities. Marijuana

175

is big business and this is their opportunity to get involved. Isn't that better than crime lords running the streets?"

By this time the crowd was getting so raucous Patricia decided it was time to leave.

"I'm glad to see the members of the Baptist Coalition are so open minded. Maybe you think shouting out opposition makes you sound intelligent, but it doesn't. The Marijuana Growers Conference will happen. Legalized marijuana is the way of the future and there's nothing you can do to stop it. Get used to it!"

With that, she left the stage, chased by loud jeers.

People on both sides of the debate held their champion up as heroes. Patricia's unexpected appearance galvanized both sides of the debate. Meanwhile, the TV stations were ecstatic. Ratings for the coverage of the confrontation were spectacular and the hits on the podcast kept going up. No one's opinion was changed by the debate, but that wasn't the goal. The goal was to boost viewership. The managers at the station looked at the numbers and were happy. And, every time it was played, Patricia's plug of the conference got viewed. Patricia was very pleased.

Milda was also pleased with her performance.

"You certainly had some fire on that stage," she said over the phone. "Do you mind if I ask what you thought of to get your anger up?"

"That was easy. I just thought about how Roger left me with all of this mess."

§§§§§

"Patricia? There's a call from a reporter with the New York Evening Star. Do you want to talk to her?"

"Sure, put her through."

Patricia looked at the flashing light on her desk phone and took a deep breath before answering.

"Patricia Kennealy. May I help you?"

"Ms. Kennealy, my name is Jo Black. I'm a science reporter with the New York Evening Star. I saw the podcast of your on-stage debate with Darius Hagerty and would like to do a follow-up story on it. Do you have some time?"

Patricia couldn't help but think 'this is it.' If this went well, she would get the big publicity she needed. She hated to admit it, but Darius had been right.

"Yes, I do. Before we begin, I would like to ensure you have Mr. Hagerty's contact information. I would not want to mischaracterize his position on the matter."

"I would appreciate that. You're right, it would make it better to include comments from both of you."

"Hold on a second and I'll get it for you."

§§§§§

Inquiries for the conference started coming in shortly after that, along with registrations. For the first time, Patricia was beginning to hope she would find a way out of the financial mess Roger left behind. She was examining the numbers when a delivery arrived for her – a dozen pink and yellow roses. The delivery man said it was from an anonymous admirer, but the note said, "A token of my appreciation."

Chapter Thirteen

As the number of conference registrations continued to increase, Patricia was optimistic they would have enough funds to cover at least most of Roger's debts, possibly even all of them. With people actually coming to this thing, she realized she needed to get serious about making plans. Over the ensuing weeks, the two women were busy on a nearly full-time basis answering queries, conducting interviews, and making arrangements. Her mother's birthday was in the middle of July and for the first time she was beginning to believe she would be able to wish her a happy birthday instead of telling her how her daughter was going into bankruptcy.

Neal had been a big help, after all. Once they had the added money, he was all on board with the conference and volunteered his assistance. At first he was merely acting as an adviser, giving the two women tips on how to set up a conference and, on occasion, pointing out mistakes. Roger had already made some arrangements, but the majority was still up in the air. Over the last weeks before the conference she and Jana, with Neal's directions and assistance, worked constantly to put the whole thing together.

One day, after Patricia asked him to come over to assist on a particular problem, the two of them were talking about the conference and she expressed how well it was going.

"I'm very thankful for your help," she told him. "This has been a real learning experience for us."

"Well, the two of you have been doing a good job. You've made mistakes, but you've recovered every time and moved on. Good job. It seems as if you're learning the business."

Patricia felt a little pride at his comments. She had worked hard and she appreciated someone noticing how she was making progress.

"I'll tell you a little secret. I'm wondering if I might not be able to do this again."

Neal expressed surprise. "Why would you want to do that?"

"Do you realize how much profit there is here? I understand now what Roger was thinking. We'll make maybe forty or fifty thousand dollars over the conference expenses. That's all going to pay off Roger's debts this time, but what about future conferences?"

179

"Future conferences? You think there's a market?" he asked.

"Yeah, I do. I haven't discussed it with John, yet. But, if I could do this maybe once a year I could raise enough money to pay for my kids' college education. That would be really wonderful."

She was looking away and didn't see the look on Neal's face.

"Yes, that would be wonderful," he said.

Neal was around a lot more after that.

§§§§§

It was a relief when the day for the conference finally arrived. She kept telling herself she just had to get through the conference and she would be done.

Jana was doing a last-minute review to ensure everything was in order when Patricia handed her an envelope.

"What's this," she asked.

"We have enough to cover the conference expenses and escrow released the money. There will be enough to pay most of Roger's debts, too. I wanted to make sure you were paid first."

Jana held the check as she gave Patricia a hug.

"Oh, thank you. This means so much to me."

"I appreciate how much you've done. I know you have a new job starting next week. You could have bailed out on me any time, but you stuck it out and I'm thankful. I could not have managed all of this without you. That's not an exaggeration."

Patricia arrived early at the hotel to ensure everything was set up and was surprised to find the conference room dark and empty, sending her to locate the customer service representative.

"Excuse me, but the conference room I had reserved is empty. My conference is scheduled to begin this morning and nothing is set up."

"Everything is fine, Mrs. Kennealy. We moved you to the larger room, just as you requested."

"I requested?"

"Yes, ma'am. Someone called up and identified himself as your representative and requested the larger conference room. He had the contract number and all of the proper contact information, so we accommodated the request. Was there a mistake?"

Thinking quickly, Patricia told him, "My apologies. In all of the hustle I forgot about that. Thank you for your help. Could you direct me to the correct room, please?"

There was no reason to blame him. She knew it wasn't his fault. As soon as he stated it was a 'he' who made the request, she knew who it was. Now, she was wondering what other surprises Neal had in store for her. As they were walking through the lobby she spotted Jana looking confused and waved at her.

"What's going on? Nothing is set up."

"Neal moved us to another room. We're on the way there now. We'll need to make corrections to the signs or no one will find us."

At first, Patricia was pleased with the new arrangements. The amount of room was nearly double and there was no doubt it would make moving around easier. But, she knew it would come at a price. Too late to do anything about it, she sighed and accepted the reality.

"What's that?" asked Jana. Patricia looked where she was pointing and saw workers setting up food servers.

The customer representative told them, "It's the breakfast buffet. I don't have anything to do with the caterers, so I'm not sure what arrangements were made. I can enquire for you, though."

Patricia smiled at him and said, "No, that won't be necessary. Thank you for all of your help. We'll be in touch if we need anything else."

After he left, Patricia turned to Jana and said, "We need to find out how many other changes Neal made. Why isn't he here? See if you can get him on the phone."

While Jana was busy doing that, Patricia searched for the catering supervisor.

"Hi! I thought we ordered a breakfast bar with some bagels and croissants. What's this?" Patricia already knew the answer, she just wanted to confirm it.

"Your representative called and changed the order."

"Let me guess. He had all of the proper information."

"Yes, that's right. Is anything wrong?"

181

"Possibly, but it isn't your fault. Could you tell me what other changes he made?"

"Sure." Referring to the paperwork he told her, "He also ordered a full lunch buffet."

"A lunch buffet?"

"Yes, ma'am. And, an open bar in the afternoon. Ma'am? Are you alright?"

Patricia felt a little light-headed, but assured the man she was fine.

"Well, maybe you should sit down. My people can handle everything here."

Patricia took his advice and sat down. That's where Jana found her, leaning forward with her head in her hands.

"Are you okay?"

"No. This is turning into a disaster. Let me guess, you couldn't get hold of Neal."

"The calls went straight to voicemail."

"That bastard!" Patricia finally sat back before telling her the news.

"I get it," Jana said. "He knows we're calling about these changes and is ignoring us."

"That's the gist of it. And, this is going to cost us thousands of dollars more. The open bar by itself will bust our budget. Do you have any idea how much booze a hundred people can drink when someone else is paying for it? No wonder he's not around anywhere."

"What do we do now?"

"We do the only thing we can. We set up the reception table, just as we planned. People will be arriving soon."

Acting more calmly than she felt, Patricia directed the helpers to their respective places as they arrived. Neal had insisted she not have any position herself and made her hire temporary help to manage the various tasks required to make a conference run smoothly. It was Patricia's role to move around and make sure everyone had what they needed to do their jobs. She quickly knew he was right. There were enough questions and loose ends to keep her busy.

Everyone, investors and presenters, were provided with a formal listing of all presentations so everyone knew what the topics were. Investors were shown to their seats

182

and the first presenters started on time. Everything was going well and Patricia, circling around, stopped to check on Jana.

"Patricia? Who are those guys?" Jana was indicating a group of six men who had entered and were making their way to the buffet. What made them stand out was the fact that, in a room full of business suits, they were wearing faded blue jeans and t-shirts. Their hair was long and shaggy and they were unshaven.

"Oh, god! It looks like we've attracted a party of homeless people coming here to scrounge a meal. I'll tell you what, there is plenty of food. Let them get something to eat and let's see what happens. Maybe they'll go away on their own."

They nervously watched as the group filled plates with food and then stood, taking in the event. Finally, one of them made their way towards the door, but instead of leaving, he went straight to the registration table.

Patricia worked to keep her composure as she asked, "Can I help you, sir?"

"I hope so. Who's in charge of this little shin-dig?"

"I am. I'm Patricia Kennealy," she replied as she held out her hand. She was hoping courtesy would defuse the situation and they would leave quietly.

The man took her hand and said, "Me and my colleagues, we heard about your deal here the other day and came all the way from California to see it. Say, weren't you the lady in that video? The one where you ripped up that preacher guy? Boy! That was great."

"Thank you. Yes, it was me. You said you came from California?" she asked in an attempt to change the subject. "That's quite a trip. But, you understand everyone here paid a registration fee?"

"Oh, yes ma'am. How much is it? Is it too late to get in?"

"Well, the registration was online, but I suppose we could let you pay by credit card. It is $500 for an investor and $1,000 for a presenter."

"I don't use credit cards. It makes it too easy for the government to track you. How about cash?"

With that, he pulled out a wad of money and counted out $6,000 in hundred dollar bills. Patricia watched with some amazement as he did this, noting he still had a large roll of bills remaining, and had to ask, "Who did you say you are?"

"I didn't. I prefer to remain anonymous, if you get my drift. But, just take it for granted we come from a big marijuana market and we're interested in finding investors. Will that work?"

Patricia looked at the mound of money he was offering her and replied, "That'll work. Enjoy yourself. A wet bar will be opening later this afternoon."

"We don't drink, but thanks anyways. By the way, we appreciate your hospitality. Lots of people would have thrown us out."

"My pleasure. We're always looking to expand the market," she said as she handed him a receipt and watched as he returned to his group.

Turning to Jana, she said, "I don't know which amazes me most. The fact that these marijuana guys are all dressed like business executives or the one that is dressed like a hippie is loaded with cash. This is one strange world we got involved with."

Everything continued to go well and she found herself making the rounds without having to do much. They had invested so much energy setting up everything it was running like a well-oiled machine. Just being available and visible was enough for most of the people they had hired. As she was working her way around the room, she saw two men who definitely didn't fit in enter the room. They were wearing sharply pressed khaki pants with light coats over button down white shirts, boots and hats. Their coats were open in front, revealing brown leather belts with a silver buckle and a Texas emblem.

"Oh, crap," she thought. "Those two are cops if I ever saw one."

The two men were surveying the room and quietly talking to each other. Occasionally, one would point something out and comment to the other. Patricia watched for a while with the hope they would simply go away, but she caught Jana's eye and could see the younger woman was watching, too. Resigning herself, Patricia made her way over to them.

"May I help you gentlemen?"

In response, they pulled their coats aside and showed their badges. Patricia immediately recognized the circle with a star in it – Texas Rangers, the criminal investigative unit of the State of Texas.

Her knees got weak as she thought about what to say next. Without batting an eye, she said, "I see. Are you here on official business, or were you looking to invest?"

184

The two officers looked at each other and laughed.

"She's tough."

"I'll say. No, ma'am. We're only taking in the sights, if you don't mind. Just curious, is all."

"We were in the lobby on some other business when we saw your sign out front and thought we would pop in to see how it's going. So, how does this work?"

Feeling relieved, she told them, "Well, we're providing a venue for people to get together. Each panel is made up of judges looking to invest money. The presenters are pitching investment ideas in the hope of finding someone to give them money. Each presenter has a strict 10-minute period to present, followed by 5 minutes for questions. We have over a hundred presenters. Even with two tables of investors, it will take two days for everyone to present. I have moderators to supervise the presentations and enforce the rules."

"And, all the opportunities have to do with growing marijuana?"

"No," she said. "But, they relate to the industry. As I'm sure you gentlemen are aware, marijuana is a gigantic industry. And, it's only going to get bigger as more and more states make it legal. Even if they only legalize it for medicinal purposes, we're still talking about many billions of dollars a year."

"What are some of the things they are pitching?"

"I've been working the room, so I haven't been able to pay that much attention. But, for instance, one guy was making a proposal about how to make marijuana grow under specific lighting. Different lighting results in different products. So, if you want marijuana to treat one kind of medical condition, you would grow it under one kind of lighting. But, if you wanted it for a different condition, you would use a different frequency of light. It turns out the frequency of light has a big impact on the final product."

"Really? I knew there were different kinds of pot out on the street, but I didn't think just changing the light would make a big difference."

"Neither did I. There're all sorts of things I'm learning today that I never would have guessed at. These guys are brilliant. They aren't a bunch of crazy pot-heads. This is serious business. Their biggest worry is appearing as if they're stoned. Some of them are

185

working so hard to not appear stoned it's a little painful. We've split the presentations into 'touching the plant' over here and over there," she waved her arm towards the panel on the other side of the room, "are the 'not touching the plant' presentations."

"But, none of this really matters if it isn't legalized. How do people feel about that?" one of the Rangers asked.

"The return on investment is so high they are willing to take the risk. It may change in the future, but people getting in right now have the chance to realize gigantic profit margins. So, tell me, how do you guys feel about legalization?"

"I'm all for it, ma'am," said one. "If pot were legal it would make our jobs a whole lot easier. We could spend our time going after bad guys instead of people selling out of their kitchens. And, if we were growing it here in the U.S., we wouldn't have to worry about the cartels."

"But, I can tell you something, ma'am," said his partner. "Not everyone here is a lab researcher. I noticed those guys over there – the ones in the jeans. That one guy with the beard is Olin Ambrosio. He's one of the biggest growers in California and the things he does are certainly not legal. We've busted a number of his shipments to Texas, but have never been able to pin anything on him. Interesting he's here." The pot grower noticed the Rangers looking at him. "Wave," he said to his partner. "It'll make him freak out." The two Rangers waved their hands in his direction and smiled. Patricia could tell the grower was uncomfortable, but he stood his ground.

"Well, thanks for the tour, ma'am. We need to be getting back to work."

After they left, Patricia walked over to Ambrosio.

"Looking for information for your cop friends?"

"What? No. Don't worry about them. They were just curious about the show."

"And, they just happened to look right at me."

"They did say they recognized you. Which is why I came over."

"I suppose you're going to ask us to leave now."

"The thought never crossed my mind. I was hoping I could get some contact information from you."

"No, thanks. I like to stay off the grid."

186

"Well, let me ask you this. Would you be interested if we had another conference? Say, in the fall, or maybe next year?"

Ambrosio looked surprised. He turned to his friends with a quizzical look. When they all nodded, he turned back to Patricia and said, "Yeah, I think we might be interested. I'll tell you what, I'll give you the information for our attorney. Send anything to him and he'll be able to get it to us. Will that work?"

"Perfectly. And tell me, do you think you would be able to spread the word?"

"About a conference?" She nodded her head. "Sure. You bet."

"That would be great. Thank you. I hope you enjoy yourselves. Oh, and be sure to check out the desserts. They're pretty scrumptious."

§§§§§

"I can't believe we did it. We actually pulled it off."

They were in the nearly empty office, enjoying a bottle of wine Patricia had taken from the conference open bar.

"I'm miffed at Neal for the changes he made without my permission," she said as she refreshed their glasses, "but that isn't going to stop me from enjoying this wine."

Exhausted from working the conference for two days, they were still pleased with the results. They raised their glasses and touched them together with a clink.

"I can't believe it went so well. We'll be able to pay off most of Roger's debts. I think I'll be stuck with some, but it will be manageable. Can you check the account balance? Now that it's done, we'll need to start writing checks."

Jana's exuberance quickly turned somber when as she looked at the computer screen.

"Patricia? Did you make a withdrawal from the account?"

"No. Why?"

"It says here the balance is $4,235."

"What? No! There should be over a hundred thousand dollars in there!"

Jana showed her the online account statement. Patricia felt the now familiar feeling of the walls falling in on her.

187

"What happened? Where did it go?"

"And, there's more. I have a notice from the bank saying the check you gave me bounced."

"Oh, my god, Jana! What happened?"

"It looks like we've been robbed."

§§§§§

"John, I was standing at the door when the bank opened this morning. I talked to the branch manager and told him what happened."

"What did they say?"

"Well, they were very concerned, I'll give them that much. They got on the phone and the computers and tracked it down. It's not good. They said I had a cashier's check mailed to a PO Box."

"Why would they say you did it?"

"Because, it was done with my password and whoever did it used my social security number and all of the correct passcodes."

"Are you saying someone stole your identity?"

"That's what it sounds like. John, we needed that money," she said, holding back the tears. "I did this conference to try and make enough money to pay off Roger's debts. Now, it's even worse than when I started. I don't even have the money to pay the conference expenses. What am I going to do now?"

"You filed a report with the bank?"

"Yes. There'll be an investigation, but they didn't sound hopeful. I at least took out the remaining money while I could and closed the account."

John was confused and dismayed. Having the burden of Roger's debts on them had been wearing on him as much as on Patricia. Plus, having to watch his wife suffer under the stress and burden had hurt, as well. Now, this disaster. He knew it didn't help, but he couldn't stop thinking about how life is just plain unfair sometimes. What had they done to deserve this?

He mustered his remaining strength and told Patricia, "It sounds like you've done all you can do for now. Why don't you come home? It's Friday. Take the weekend to think about it and start fresh on Monday. Can you do that?"

"I guess so. I don't know what else to do right now. I'm so tired, John. I'm supposed to be celebrating. Instead, it feels as if the whole world has collapsed on me."

"I know, honey. Come home. Okay?"

"Alright. I'm on my way."

Before she started the drive she took the time to sit in her car and cry.

Chapter Fourteen

Patricia dragged herself home, exhausted and demoralized. She had worked so hard to overcome the obstacles, only to have it all stolen. The battle was wearing her down and she knew it. This latest development left her feeling completely defeated when she should have been celebrating success.

It was the middle of the afternoon, but all she wanted to do was crawl in bed and sleep until the world ended. Or, longer. She was so weary she didn't even think about how John's car was in the garage this early in the day until she walked in and found him waiting for her.

He gave her a hug and kiss before saying, "We're going away for the weekend. I gave the kids pizza money and instructions to not burn the house down, so we're free to hit the road."

She was dismayed at what she heard and was about to object, but he cut her off as she opened her mouth. "Uh, uh. I know. You're exhausted and you only want to relax. But I also know you'll never do that here. You'll be reading documents and calling people all weekend. I've already packed you a bag. I'll do the driving so you can take a nap."

"John, I need to find the missing money."

"I know. But you've done all you can for right now. You can follow up on Monday. You can't think clearly right now. You have to step back and let your mind clear. Listen, you've done everything you can do. You took care of the funeral, the apartment and even the conference. You've taken care of everyone except yourself. You need a break. If you keep going like this, you'll have a breakdown."

"Can I ask where we're going?"

"Fredericksburg."

She stopped and thought about it when he said that. Fredericksburg was one of their favorite places. They had gone there for their honeymoon and had been regular visitors since. The Texas Hill Country was the place where good little Texans go when they die. If they're lucky, they don't have to wait that long.

"I thought it'd be nice to visit the town before the weather gets too nice and the tourists take over."

"John, we're tourists."

"I mean all of those other tourists. It's okay for us to be there."

Patricia could only shake her head in amazement at his logic.

"Okay, but let me look at that bag you packed. I don't trust a man to do my packing, even if I have been married to him for over twenty years. And, I want to grab something real quick."

She swapped a few items, but was generally pleased with the job John had done. Fifteen minutes later, they were pulling out of the garage and heading south. Exhaustion won the battle with Patricia and she was asleep in minutes.

Normally, the trip from Cisco to Fredericksburg would take about three hours. John headed south on Highway 377 to Brownwood, where he connected with U.S. Highway 110 and headed straight towards Fredericksburg. He was in no rush to get anywhere. He was concerned about his wife and intended this to be a leisurely trip. She was working herself too hard and the stress was showing. He wanted to make this as much of a fun and relaxing trip for her as he could. He was pretty sure she had earned it.

Highway 110 took them from the plains of northern central Texas into the rolling, limestone terrain of the Llano Uplift, a region dominating the area west of Austin and north of San Antonio. Lyndon Baines Johnson grew up here and would bring world leaders to his ranch just outside of Stonewall. The beautiful, enchanting terrain belied the harsh living, resulting in a sparse population for most of Texas' history. Only in modern times, when people didn't rely on the land for their livelihood as much, did the population begin to boom. Today, vineyards and wineries were becoming a billion-dollar industry for the region.

John saw the sign announcing they had reached Holmes County. Below it was a sign reading, "Entering the No Stress Zone." He knew from the other side, visible as you were leaving, the sign read, "Returning to the Real World. Best Wishes."

Patricia sat up and looked around, getting her bearings before asking, "Where are we?"

"We're coming up on Dog Run. I thought you might want to stop for a break."

192

She smiled as she thought of the little town nestled in middle of the Nation of Nowhere.

"That's sounds good. Do you think it's too early to get a drink?"

"I was planning on it," he said, smiling at her.

People who visited Dog Run for the first time would decide within minutes if they never wanted to see it again, or move there and settle down. It was that kind of place. Almost equidistant to the more populated towns of Fredericksburg, Llano and Mason, it was in a sort of Shangri-La-like valley on the Lucia River. Driving through the town square, past one of the most majestic county courthouses in Texas, they pulled up in front of one their favorite stops in all of the Hill Country – The Get Away To.

Entering The Get Away To was a surreal experience. The pub's owner, Matt Silpert, had visited Ireland and enjoyed himself so much he wanted to bring some of it home. While he was there, he learned a certain building had been condemned as unsafe and was about to be torn down. In the building was an old, traditional Irish pub. Matt managed to purchase the pub before demolition and had it carefully taken apart. Every piece of the pub was lovingly disassembled, numbered and shipped to Dog Run, where it was reassembled in perfect order inside a building Matt had had built to the exact specifications of the pub. As a result, patrons walked through the Texas sun across the caliche parking lot and entered Ireland as they passed through the door. A genuine Irish pub sitting in the center of the Texas Hill Country. First-time visitors would sometimes look back through the door to make sure Texas was still outside.

The sign near the front said the name came from people saying they needed to get away from things. Matt decided if they were getting away from something, they needed something to get away to - the Get Away To. And, he worked hard to make sure it lived up to the name. The rest of the world ceased to exist when you walked through its door.

John and Patricia had immediately fallen in love with it the first time they visited.

The interior of the pub was dark and cool, a welcome break even in late April. It was mid-afternoon and the crowd was thin as they made their way across the comfortably furnished room. Matt was washing glasses behind the bar and looked up as they approached.

"John and Patricia! What a surprise. It's been too long."

They weren't surprised he remembered them and was able to recall their names. It was one his gifts and one of the things that made the Get Away To special. People came to see Matt, if for no other reason.

They exchanged hugs and handshakes before John and Patricia took a seat at the bar.

"What can I get you two?" Matt asked.

John looked over at Patricia before answering, "I think we would both love a nice Guinness. And, can we see a menu? We haven't had anything since breakfast."

They placed their order and Matt passed it to the kitchen. With a Guinness in hand, Patricia knocked mugs with her husband before leaning over and kissing him.

"Thank you. This was a great idea."

"I'm just trying to take care of my girl," he replied.

"And, you do a good job."

Patricia felt a surge of affection and snuggled up closer to John.

"Where are you guys heading?" Matt asked.

John turned from Patricia and answered, "Nowhere in particular. We were heading to Fredericksburg, but we don't have any kind of agenda. We're just taking the weekend off to relax."

"There's nowhere better to relax than Dog Run. Why don't you guys spend the night here and go into F-burg tomorrow," using the common nickname for the nearby town.

John looked at Patricia, who nodded her approval, "We might just do that. We don't have any real reason to push on tonight."

After eating, they walked out to the town square. A bed and breakfast located on the square had a room available and, after checking in, they stretched out on the luxurious king-sized bed and took a nap.

By the time they woke up it was nearly dark. John found Patricia looking out the window with a thoughtful look.

"What's the matter?"

"I'm ready. This is the place."

"Ready for what?"

In response, she held up a container for him to see.

"I grabbed this before we left. Can we walk down to the river?"

John understood immediately and silently nodded his head. Crossing Margot Street, the main street in and out of town, they walked into the town park occupying the flood plain between the town square and the Lucia River. The hillside was steep, but the path was a good one and they had no problems making their way in the fading light. The full moon was just coming up as they approached the banks of the river and they could hear coyotes howling up the river.

"Those sound pretty close," she commented.

John listened to the howling before answering, "I don't think those are coyotes. That's a group of people howling at the moon."

"Ah, yes. Some real party animals. How appropriate."

John softly laughed, "Yeah, it kinda is."

By this time, they had reached the edge of the river and were standing on some rocks overlooking the gently swirling waters. The Lucia was a spring-fed river with a fairly constant level, only occasionally swelling from flood waters. The spring rainy season had started, but it had been dry for several days and the river was quiet. Together, they sat quietly on the granite rocks as the moon rose and the air began to cool down. Above them was a house upon the hill. The moon was lying still. Shadows of the trees were witnessing the wild breeze.

"River flow, on and on it goes," John softly said.

"He said he wanted me to spread his ashes somewhere beautiful. He didn't say anything more than that. I decided this was the place."

"It's a good choice. I don't think he ever made it out here, but I'm pretty sure he would be happy with it."

With tears welling up, all she could do is nod as she opened up the container and, with the crowd up stream howling their approval, she slowly poured the ashes into the water. After a few moments, John took the container from her and used the river to wash out any remains that might not have fallen out.

"Goodbye, Roger."

With that, she indicated she was ready to go.

195

As they approached the Get Away To, they could hear music softly wafting across the square.

...

She's as sweet as Dublin Dr. Pepper,
Pure cane sugar keeps me coming back for more,
She's as sweet as Dublin Dr. Pepper,
I get my loving right on time,
10, 2 and 4

...

"Just another Friday night in Dog Run," John said.

They found a group of people sitting on the porch enjoying drinks and dinner. Several people recognized them from previous visits and invited them to join the group, which they were happy to do. What followed was nothing special, just an evening visiting with friends enjoying music while swapping stories and jokes.

As the evening wore on, John was pleased to see the strained look in his wife's face being gradually replaced with a smile and laughter. She would occasionally check her phone for calls before putting it back in her purse. But, he noticed she was doing it less frequently. Staying over, he knew, was the right thing to do. Dog Run really was the No Stress Zone.

It was getting late when the group broke up. John took Patricia by the hand and led her back to the B&B. Soon, she was cuddled up to him and quickly fell into a deep sleep. He stayed awake for a while, watching her as she slept before drifting off himself.

§§§§§

After breakfast, they continued the trip to Fredericksburg. It was a short drive from Dog Run to the German settlement and they were there well before lunch. They went sightseeing along Main Street, enjoying people watching and getting lunch in one of the many German restaurants. John noticed how Patricia would get a glazed look at times and would check her phone, but she slowly relaxed and the stress lines in her face were beginning to smooth out. It was mid-afternoon before they finally went looking for a

196

place to stay for the night, locating a nice B&B they both liked near the town square. He suggested they take a short nap and she didn't object.

The day had been warm with the sunshine, but it was nearly sundown and cooling quickly by the time they awoke. The B&B was only a couple of blocks from Main Street and they decided to walk, enjoying the beautiful evening weather. They made their way to the nearby town square and decided to do a little exploring. In all of their previous visits, they had never taken the time to look at it closely. This, they decided, seemed like a perfect time to fix that oversight.

Known as Marktplatz, the Market Square, it was built with the original settlement and is used to host festivals, concerts and an ice skating rink in the holiday season. It also offers a public gathering space, a playground for children and places for a picnic. It is a big draw during Oktoberfest and festively decorated for Christmas. Tonight, it was just a nice town square.

Located in the center of the square was the octagonal-shaped Vereins Kirche, the Society Church, which was built soon after the settlers arrived. It served as the town's first church, the first school, the town hall, and as a fort in case of attack. There was a garden to one side. Patricia pointed at it and said, "Let's see what's in there."

The garden was dominated by manicured bushes, but in a clear area they found a statue of a man on one knee handing a pipe to a sitting Comanche chief. Another Native American was standing to the side, watching the proceeding.

They weren't alone. There was an old man looking at the statute, dressed in a long, black coat and white, straw cowboy hat. John estimated him to be in his 70s. They greeted the man before turning their attention to the statue. Together, John and Patricia looked at it before John asked her, "What do you think that's about?"

"I don't know," she replied.

The old man spoke without looking up, "That's John O. Meusebach, founder of Fredericksburg, and a Comanche war chief, making a peace treaty."

John was impressed. "I didn't think it was possible to make a treaty with the Comanche."

The old man nodded in agreement.

"Not many could pull it off. But, Meusebach was an interesting guy. He was born in Prussia as Baron Otfried Hans von Meusebach. He renounced his title when he came to the US and changed his name. He led a group of German settlers out here and founded Fredericksburg in 1846.

"This was very wild country in those days and life was very hard. People worked all day just to survive. By 1846, Manhattan had over 300,000 people and Harvard had been teaching students for over 200 years. But, this area was still true frontier. The people back east didn't believe the stories they heard and thought it was all made up. But, it was true.

"In addition to drought and flood and all the other things nature threw at them, there was a constant threat from the Indians in the area, mostly the Comanche. A conflict with them would have meant the end of the settlement, maybe even the people in it. Meusebach decided to deal with the situation and met with the Comanche to negotiate a treaty. He had the ideal personality to negotiate the treaty and they agreed to talk. In February of 1847, Meusebach and several government people met with the Comanche some thirty miles north of here.

"The Comanche camp had about 150 tents and a thousand horses. The three great Comanche chiefs brought their entire tribes, including the women and children. In the morning, the Comanche spread buffalo hides in a circle in front of their tents. The chiefs and their best warriors sat on one side and the Americans on the other. In the center was a pile of tobacco and a pipe. The Indians would puff on the pipe and pass it around. Meusebach made a proposal and the chiefs said they would consider it. The next day, they met again and the chiefs announced they would accept the proposal. They celebrated with a feast that night and then everyone broke camp in the morning. The treaty was signed a few days later and was essential to settling this area.

"The treaty turned out to be so favorable for both sides it was the foundation of eleven Texas counties. It's considered to be the only treaty between white settlers and Native Americans that was never broken. Funny how things happen." He continued, "All he wanted to do is make things safe for his settlement."

198

John and Patricia had quietly listened to the old man telling the tale. Finally, John said, "That's a great story. But, I thought the peace pipe was something Hollywood invented."

"Oh no, it was real. Hollywood certainly abused the idea, but the Indian tribes were well known to share tobacco as a token of peace."

"Do you know who these chiefs are?" he asked, pointing at the statue.

"The one sitting down is Chief Santa Ana, also known as Chief Santana. He was one of the greatest chiefs of his era. The one standing is symbolic and represents all of the other chiefs who participated in the treaty."

"Are you from this area?" John asked.

"Originally, but I left when I was a young man to make my fortune, without success. About twenty years ago I was wondering what to do with my life when a friend of mine told me a story. When I lived in Dallas I played poker with a group of people. One of them was this priest I had known for years. He told me about how he and a friend nearly lost their lives in a storm and said it changed them both. He said it made him realize you need to devote yourself to the important things in life. I decided being with family was more important than a fortune. So, I came home. Funny thing is I got involved with the new wine industry in the region and made my fortune with it."

"You seem very familiar with the treaty story," Patricia remarked.

"John Meusebach was my great-great-grandfather. I'm Oscar Meusebach. Grandpa John told the story to my grandfather when he was a boy and grandpa passed it on to me when I was a boy. We still have Grandpa John's journals. Well, nice meeting you folks. I hope you enjoy the rest of your evening."

With a tip of his hat to Patricia, the old man turned away and walked off into the night.

"Wow! That was amazing," remarked John. Patricia could only nod in agreement.

§§§§§

Only one block west from the square was Hondo's. John and Patricia knew it was hard to find a better music venue with food that good and music that's cooking, too. A

199

classic Texas honky-tonk, it was the kind of place you would expect to find a young George Strait, Waylon Jennings or Willie Nelson. Or, maybe, Bob Wills and the Texas Playboys. And, who knows, maybe one of the bands playing there now will have that kind of reputation someday. Tonight, it was a little-known C&W band, honing their skills by playing their way across the state in hopes of someday hitting it big.

They ordered their meals and found a place to sit. By the time the band started, it was getting crowded. For the next few hours, John and Patricia spent their time dancing and forgetting the troubles that had rained on their shoulders since Roger died.

On the way back to the B&B, John spoke about the man they had met in the town square earlier.

"The more I think about him the more convinced I am the priest friend he spoke of was Father Francis, Roger's friend," he said.

"Maybe. I'm sure he's not the only poker-playing priest in Dallas. There's probably a bunch of them."

John nodded in agreement.

"Sure, but if so, that would mean he played poker at Roger's and his story takes on added relevance as a result. Think of how his great-great grandfather had been faced with overwhelming obstacles and had overcome them. Our problems pale in comparison to what those settlers faced. We don't have to worry about Indian attacks. Our lives don't depend on the whims of the weather. No matter what happened with Roger's estate, we're still going to have food to eat, a home to sleep in, medical care and clean running water."

Patricia thought about it. Even if he was mistaken about the priest, the message was still the same.

"Oscar Meusebach was right," she told him. "I need to focus on the important things."

§§§§§

Back in the B&B, when they got ready for bed, John admired the nightgown she wore with her red hair flowing over her shoulders, illuminated only by the moonlight coming in through the window.

"Wow. That's really something. I know I didn't pack that one."

"No, you didn't. That's why I don't let a man pack for me. It looks even better lying on the floor."

She was no longer the flawless young woman he married. Time and childbirth had taken their toll on her body. But, this woman here had traveled the road of experience with him as they made a life together. John placed his hands on her hips and slowly moved them up to her waist, feeling her warmth. His gaze moved up until he was looking her in the eyes.

"You are one beautiful woman," he whispered in the dark.

With a smile, she took his hand and led him to the bed.

§§§§§

She didn't know what time it was when she woke up, but it was still dark and the lack of noise told her it was in the early hours. John continued to sleep next to her, lightly breathing. She quietly got out of bed, being careful not to disturb her husband. It was chilly in the room and she put on a sweater to warm herself. She hadn't packed a bathrobe, so she grabbed some towels from the bathroom and used them to keep her legs and feet warm as she curled up in one of the chairs.

She looked out the window into the darkness. Not too far away, a hoot owl was calling in the hope of finding a mate. There was little other noise.

Something had bothered her. In her sleep, her brain had continued working, processing all it knew. It eventually reached a conclusion so disturbing it was what had woke her from her exhausted, but sound, slumber. As she sat in the darkness, she realized what it was.

Neal Dent was a crook.

§§§§§

201

"Are you sure?" John asked over breakfast. Patricia had patiently waited until they were at the restaurant and had ordered. They were waiting for their meals and had a few minutes in private. She told him of her realization of the previous night.

"Yes. Everything fits. I always wondered why Roger picked me to do all of this. I don't know anything about running a business. Why not get one of his business friends to do it?"

She stirred her coffee as she looked out the window at the traffic with cars parking headfirst.

"That was a red flag. They were lifelong friends, but Roger didn't turn to him when he needed someone," John observed.

"Right. I should have been more suspicious, but I've been overwhelmed. I let things get by."

"You can't be blamed, honey. You've been doing all anyone could possibly ask of you. I can tell you this, Roger picked the right person. I can't imagine anyone else would take care of his affairs the way you have."

She smiled at him and squeezed his hand before continuing.

"Thanks, but I may have screwed up. I think I let the fox into the henhouse. What occurred to me last night is how Neal had access to the office. The account information was in there. I'm sure one of those documents had my social security number. It would be easy to go online and order a cashier's check after that. Then, he could just sit on it until things settle down. I even know why he did it."

"A hundred thousand dollars seems like plenty of motive."

"Not for a greedy person. Not if you can get even more. Neal wants it all. He knew I needed that money to pay Roger's debts. He'll offer to assume the debts in exchange for the rights to the conference. By taking the money, he not only managed to get the money, but he forced me into a corner where I'll have no choice but to give it to him in exchange for him covering the debts. He thinks I'll be so grateful for the offer I'll cheerfully turn it all over to him and he'll act like the true, sympathetic friend who's remaining loyal to his dead friend. Then, he'll default on the debts and pay pennies on the dollar to settle."

202

"You think he wants to hold a series of conferences." It was statement, not a question.

"Yes. John, he could make nearly $50,000 profit every year off a series of conferences. That explains why he was so helpful. Why he went to so much trouble to help make it a success."

"It sounds like you've learned a lot about the business world."

"Unfortunately, most of those lessons have been painful," she said as she took a sip from her coffee.

"What are you going to do? Do you have enough to go to the police?"

"I don't want to do that, even if I did. That would just tie everything up in court for years to come. What I want is to close this all out. I want to put Roger to rest and for us to get on with our lives."

"What if you can't find the money? Have you thought about that?"

"Yes. The reason I'm so sure that's Neal plan is because I'm the one who suggested it. The idea of a series of conferences was my idea. I told Neal about how much I've learned and all of the contact information I've managed to acquire. I wouldn't have any problem contacting the right people next time. The reviews were really good and I know a bunch of deals were made. I think I could even get Jana to help me out on the side."

"You sound as if you've thought it out."

"I have, I admit it. I was thinking it might be something to do to get money for the college funds. It occurred to me once a year wouldn't be too much of a burden. I think I could do that without too much stress."

"But, you know what? I would never have realized any of this if you hadn't made me take the weekend off. You're right. I would have spent the whole weekend reading reports and talking to people on the phone. I had to step back and take a breather. I had to give all of the stuff in my head a chance to sort itself out without people constantly calling and nagging me. Now that I think about it, I'm surprised I haven't been receiving a bunch of calls."

She noticed John's sheepish look when she said that.

"John? What did you do?" she asked as she reached for her phone.

"Well, I wanted you to relax. So, I kind of put it in airline mode. By accident."

"By accident?" she asked in alarm.

"You know, honey, the conference is over, you've done the memorial service. There isn't anything you can do until tomorrow. They've waited this long to hear from you. They can wait a few more hours. We'll be home this afternoon and you can go back into stress mode. But, right now, I would really like it if you would just put the phone back in your purse and enjoy the rest of the day with me."

She paused while an internal fight between Angry and Thankful raged. Eventually, Thankful won out – with an honorable mention from Angry. She put the phone back in her purse and looked at him. Out of guilt, he didn't return her gaze.

"Thank you, John. I love you," is all she had to say about it.

§§§§§

Patricia resisted the urge to take her phone off airplane mode during the return drive. While John was letting the kids know they were home, Patricia checked her voicemail and emails. John came into the room just as she was putting the phone down.

"Any calls?"

"Two."

"Who from?"

"A couple of the investors. They thought the conference was such a success they want me to do another one in the fall."

Interlude

All marriages hit rough patches, she thought during the drive from Cisco to Dallas. The question was whether this was just a patch or was it something more serious. Patricia had come to the conclusion this was one of the latter cases. She and John had been growing apart and it had reached the point where all they did was fight, even in front of the children. Tired and depressed, she turned to the person that had always given her sound advice over the years – Roger Tucci.

"I'm going to ask John for a divorce," she said without preamble as she met him at his apartment.

Roger merely nodded his head a few times before replying, "You should. A man like that doesn't deserve a woman like you."

"What do you mean?"

"You're beautiful and intelligent. Men will be lining up for you. Any man that would beat his wife should be in a prison, not a marriage."

"No! No! He never beat me. Why would you think that? He's never lifted a hand to me."

"Well, then he must be cheating on you. Clearly, he doesn't value what a wonderful woman you are. I know I would."

"What are you talking about? No, he is not cheating on me."

"It must be drinking, then. Or, gambling?"

She saw what he was doing now.

"No, he doesn't have a drinking problem and he never gambles."

"Mean to the children?"

"He's a wonderful father."

"Lousy in bed?"

She didn't answer.

"Ah. The spark has gone out of the relationship."

"That's part of it. We hardly ever make love anymore and when we do, it's just routine. But, that's only the beginning. Everything between us has been like that for months now. Routine, with no spark. We've grown apart."

205

"Months? You're quitting your marriage after only a few months of trouble?"

"No. We've gone through this before. What else can I do?"

"Why don't you begin by eliminating the things you can't do and see what remains. Have you considered marriage counseling?"

"We did that before and it helped for a while, but then we were right back where we started."

"Find him a lover?"

"Roger!"

"I'm just going through your options. Have you considered getting a lover yourself?"

"This isn't helping!"

"Lovers are out. Do you want to leave the kids and start a new life?"

"No."

"So, you want to take the kids from their father, the one you already said was wonderful to them."

"No. I don't want to do that, either," she sighed.

"Are you sure this isn't your fault?"

"What do you mean?"

"You have said nothing but wonderful things about John. Your problems all seem to be starting in the bedroom. Are you sure it's all John? It takes two people to tango, you know. Are you dancing, or are you passing the time?"

She realized she had been sitting for a long moment, lost in thought, when Roger said, "When was the last time you initiated the love making? How many times have you turned him down when he was interested?"

She sat silently, guiltily looking out the window.

"It seems we may have narrowed it down."

"Well, what do I do now?"

"Isn't it obvious?"

"Are you saying I need to be sexy? If I become some sex goddess all of our problems will go away?"

"Probably not, but it will take away the source of some of them. And, if you reduce the tension, it will make it easier to deal with the other issues."

"But, how do I make it spicy again after all these years."

Roger walked over to his book case and handed her a book when he returned.

"The Kama Sutra?" she asked. "You've got to be kidding!"

"Why? You think we're doing anything that hasn't been done for thousands of years? Besides, although it's frequently thought of as a guide for creative sexual positions, in reality, only about twenty percent of it is about sexual positions. The majority of the book is about the philosophy and theory of love, what triggers desire, what sustains it, how and when it is good or bad. It sounds to me you can use some of that. What other options do you have at this point?"

"None, I guess," she admitted as she opened the book and blushed at what she saw. And yet, she couldn't stop looking, either. She could do some of those, she thought as she turned the pages.

"See? Once you narrowed it down it was pretty easy. Get rid of the things you can't do and look at the things you can. Keep the book. Girl, you've gotta love your man. Take him by the hand and make him understand."

She gave him a quick kiss on the cheek and left. She sat in the truck for a while, just thinking, before she made up her mind. It took her a while to find the store she needed, but she was soon back on the road to Cisco.

When John got home that evening he found the children were gone. He was in the bedroom, changing out of his work clothes, when Patricia entered. She took him by the hand and asked him to sit on the edge of the bed with her.

"Where are the kids?" he asked.

"They're staying with friends tonight. I wanted to be alone with you."

This, he thought, was the talk he had been afraid was coming. Instead, she put her arms around him and kissed him.

"I love you, John. I apologize for not showing it lately. I'm going to be better and I want to show you how much I love you. Why don't you get cleaned up and come in to dinner. I fixed your favorite. Then, after dinner, I have something I bought today that I want to show you."

207

With another kiss, she got up and walked out of the room, pausing at the door to look over her shoulder and give him a naughty smile.

She never told him about her conversation with Roger, even years later.

Chapter Fifteen

"What are my options, Stan?"

Patricia had called her lawyer, Stan Woosley first thing Monday morning and set up an appointment. Previously, she had gotten into a mess because she hadn't consulted with him before acting. She wasn't going to make that mistake twice.

"You don't have many. The documents all say you were the one doing the withdrawal."

"If I did the withdrawal, where's the money?"

"It was withdrawn as a cashier's check. It could be anywhere. The evidence I've seen so far doesn't indicate anyone but you. You're convinced this Neal Dent fellow stole it?"

"Positive. He's the only one who could. Somehow, he got hold of the account information and my social security number while we were working together. He'd be able to go online and take care of everything without providing any ID. He could have even done it on the office computer when I was out of the room."

"That would be hard to prove. I'm not sure there's anything you can do about it. We can investigate, but unless we can come up with some hard evidence, it looks like he'll get away with it. All he has to do is claim you're the one that took the money and the evidence will back him up."

"But, Stan. We're talking about $100,000."

"I'm sorry there isn't more I can tell you."

"Okay. I was pretty much braced for that. But, there's one last thing. Take a look at this," she said as she handed him a folder. It was the one open business deal she and Jana found while cleaning out his office. "I found this in Roger's records when I was cleaning out his files. I may be grasping at straws, but this is my last hope."

Patricia sat silently, hoping for the best, as Stan read through the thin file.

Finally, he looked up with a smile. "I think you have something here. I'll draw up some papers."

§§§§§

"Neal, I'm in real trouble. Someone stole my identity and cleaned out the conference account. All of the money is gone and I can't pay Roger's bills. Can we meet?"

"Oh, Patricia! I'm so sorry to hear that. After all of your hard work I can't believe this could happen. Certainly we can meet. I'm free all afternoon. Why don't you come over after lunch. Will that work?"

"Thank you, Neal. I'll see you this afternoon."

As he hung up he couldn't help but smile.

"Exactly as I expected," he thought.

§§§§§

As she hung up the phone Patricia couldn't help but smile.

"Exactly as I expected," she thought.

"Now, it's my turn, you bastard."

§§§§§

Neal looked up as his secretary led Patricia into his office and welcomed her.

Patricia took the seat he indicated and waited for the secretary to leave.

"It's really bad, Neal. I told you what happened. Someone got into the conference account and stole nearly all of the money. I can't pay Roger's bills anymore."

"How much was taken?" he asked.

"$100,000"

Neal whistled when he heard the number.

"That's a lot of money. Any idea where it went?"

"No. They used my identity to log into the account and ordered a cashier's check. There's no way to trace it. Now, I don't know what to do. I was hoping you might be able to give me some advice, being Roger's friend and all."

"I've thought about it since you called this morning and I might have a solution. I think I can cover the debts, but I would need some way to recoup the expenses. What would you say to signing over the rights to the conference in exchange for me paying all of Roger's debts?"

"You'd do that?" she asked innocently.

"Roger and I were friends for years. He helped me out a couple of times so I'd be proud to help him out now. If you want, I can draw up the papers this afternoon and you'd be free of any more problems."

"Wow, Neal! That's so generous. I just have to wonder, what are you going to do with the $100,000 you stole?"

"What are you talking about? Are you joking?"

"Not at all. There are only three people who could have gotten into that account – Jana, me – and you. We didn't do it, so that leaves only you. We know what you did, Neal. Did you really think you would get away with it?"

"You're crazy! I didn't do anything. If you're going to make accusations, then our business is done. I was being generous because you're Roger's friend and I wanted to help out. But, if this is the way I'm going to be treated then we're done."

"Let me tell you what's going to happen next. You're going to agree to pay all of Roger's debts and I'm going to keep the conference rights." Neal had acted exactly as she expected. She was getting excited at the prospect of snapping the trap shut and there was no stopping her now.

"I told you, Patricia. Our business is done. I have nothing more to say to you."

"Oh, I think you do." She handed him a document before continuing. "This is a contract that says you will pay all of the conference expenses, Jana's salary – with a bonus – and all of Roger's debts. It also covers the remaining funds in the bank account and the cash payments I received at the conference from the late attendees. That money comes to me to pay my expenses."

He laughed as he tossed it back to her, unread. "I'm not signing anything. Now, get out."

"Fine. Then, I'm calling in the loan you owe Roger's estate." She was smiling now. Like a shark, she could smell the blood and was closing in for the kill. All of the

211

stress, all of the worries, all of the grief, it was all coming to the fore and she wasn't going to hold back.

"What loan?"

"Roger loaned you $50,000. You never made a single payment on that loan and it is still open. With the compound interest, it now amounts to over $250,000. I expect full payment." She showed him a file folder. "Roger kept excellent records. It's all right here. The original is with my attorney and he's ready to move as soon as I give him the word."

"Well, you won't be getting any of that money," he said, clearly not as confident as before.

"That's okay. I'll file a lawsuit to retrieve the money. I'll seize your assets. And, when we start doing discovery and depositions I'm sure we'll find a lot of things you don't want found, including a cashier's check for $100,000."

"What if you do? You don't think I deserve to be paid for my work? Do you think I worked for free?"

"There was never any discussion about payment, so the answer is 'yes,' I do think you were working for free and that's what I'll tell the court. But, that isn't important. What's important is that the check will be evidence you engaged in identity theft. You used my name, my social security number and my passcodes to get into the account. That's a federal crime, Neal. You'll go to prison for it. And, how many other crimes have you committed? Are you all up-to-date on your taxes? Oh, I'm really looking forward to tearing your financials apart. All sorts of people will want to know about what we're going to find. Especially the IRS, I'm sure."

Pouncing on Neal was so therapeutic she could feel all of the stress leaving her body and she wanted more. She was completely in control and she knew it. All of the pain and stress was coming to the surface and causing the adrenaline to rush. She was merely dragging it out for maximum pleasure.

Neal was sweating by this time, angrily shouting at her, "You don't know who you're dealing with here! Do you really think I'll let you see my financial records? What kind of idiot are you?"

"I'm the idiot in charge of Roger's estate! That gives me the authority to do everything I threatened," she said.

212

"That's because you've been sleeping with him all these years."

This was just enough to push Patricia over the edge. Circling around the end of the desk she launched herself at Dent. He put his arms up to defend himself but it wasn't enough and she knocked him to the floor, still seated in his chair. With a demonic look, she grabbed his tie and pulled it tight. He fought back, but she put her knees on his chest and pushed down with all her weight.

"Listen to me, you scumbag! I'm tired of your games!" She still pulled on his tie but let him breathe. A dead Neal wouldn't help her any. "This is what's going to happen. You're going to sign that contract and you're going to pay all of those debts. Understand me? If you don't I'll go to the police and turn you in."

"Turn me in for what?" he asked as he struggled to get his breath.

"Embezzlement! Identify theft! You took money out of an account using my name and social security number. You took money out of that account for your own use. That's a felony! By the time I get done with you your reputation will be in the toilet! It's your choice, pay now or pay big now. There's no 'later' this time. When I show the police the loan documents, that will be enough for them to get a search warrant."

It was all questionable if she could carry through with her threat, but she was hoping a guilty mind would convince Neal to believe her. She finally let him loose and got up, calmly smoothing her skirt as she walked back to the front of the desk and sat down.

Dent picked up his chair as he said, angrily, "You crazy bitch! I'll see you in jail for this! That was assault and battery. I don't have to stand for that!"

Patricia reached out so quickly Dent thought she was going to attack him again and flinched. Instead, she grabbed the phone and held it up to him.

"Fine! Call the police right now! I'll confess to everything. And, while I'm at it, I'll tell them the rest of the story, too. Is that what you want? Identify theft is only one of the crimes you've committed." She tore the phone loose and threw it at him, bouncing it off his face and giving him a bloody lip.

"Now, sign the document or I go to the police!"

He wiped the blood from his mouth and straightened his coat.

"I want time to think about this before I sign anything."

213

"Fine! You have 60 seconds. I would've given you thirty, but I want to watch you squirm," she said as she checked her watch.

"What? You really are out of your mind! I want more than that! I need days."

"You know the drill, Neal. Consider your options and throw out the ones you can't do. Are you really going to let me go to the police?"

"You're bluffing! You don't have anything on me!"

Patricia calmly announced, "There isn't even a hint of a bluff in what I'm saying, Neal. My lawyer is standing by," she said, checking her watch. "Forty-five seconds and I'm out of here. Tick, tock."

"Listen, Roger went around thinking with his dick. We all know that. His business is so complicated it will take months to straighten it out."

"How's it feel to know you're not as good as another man's penis? Thirty seconds." She looked Neal in the eye as she swung the contract between two fingers like a pendulum. "Tick. Tick. Tick. Twenty-five seconds."

"I don't have that kind of money!"

"Shut up, Neal! We both know you took a hundred thousand dollars out of the account!"

"I want the rest of the money, then."

"No, Neal. That's mine. It'll pay for my expenses and, if anything's left, I might take my family on a vacation. They've earned it. They've been left without a wife and mother most of this time. My mother's birthday is coming up in mid-July, maybe I'll take her along. Happy Birthday, Mom."

"Will you go away if I sign? What about the loan?"

"It'll be forgiven once I confirm payment on all debts. No reneging. But there's a catch. If you slander me with stories that I was sleeping with Roger ever again, I'll be back. Understand? I never slept with him and you better not even insinuate that I did. I want to be sure you can do it, so say it right now. Get used to it! Say it!"

He looked at her as the sweat beaded on his upper lip and said, "You never slept with Roger. I'm sure of it."

"Good! Now, sign the document and we don't need to see each other ever again."

Dent took the pen she offered him and signed both documents where indicated.

She put her watch away before picking up one copy and putting it in her purse. "I'd say it was a pleasure, but it wasn't. If I ever hear from you again it better be for something important." With that, she turned and walked out without waiting for a response.

She was very composed as she made her way out of the office. The elevator was crowded as she got on but she didn't really notice. She watched the indicator showing the floors as they descended and thought about how they reflected the conversation she had just had.

"Ten floors. It's counting down, Neal. Tick. Tick. Tick. Sign or I'm out of here. Only five floors remaining, the clock's ticking. What's that? You'll sign? Good because we're at the first floor. Times up."

She had never felt so empowered.

As the elevator stopped her thoughts turned to going home to her husband. With a slight smile, she thought about a certain store she knew about and decided she needed to make a detour on her way out of town. She was beautiful and felt that way.

The doors opened and she stepped out, completely unaware of how the other people in the elevator had been watching her and stood aside to let her leave first, her red hair flowing behind her. As she walked away, one of the men quietly said, "That is one beautiful woman."

Everyone else nodded their heads in agreement.

First Interlude

Roger Tucci watched the woman stretch out on the bed. She was 49 years old, but very sexy. It never entered his 17-year old mind that his first lover would be a woman nearly three times his age. And, what a lover. He had seen her in the neighborhood for years, but it wasn't until yesterday that he ever gave her much thought. As it turned out, she had thought a lot about him and she finally decided to act on the thoughts, calling him in for a made-up chore before seducing him.

"Oh, Roger, you beautiful boy. That was great yesterday. Even better than I had hoped."

"I was good?" the teenager asked hopefully. He wanted reassurance he had satisfied his first woman.

"Yes, you were. And, I'm going to teach you how to be better. I'm going to teach you how to make love to a woman like men seldom do. When I'm done with you, women will be lining up to be your lover."

Roger liked what he was hearing. Just the thought of women wanting to get in his bed was enough to get him aroused and he climbed onto the bed with the woman. He embraced her and she gave him a long, passionate kiss.

"I'll teach you how to act, how to talk, how to dress. I want you to dress in purple shirts from now on. It brings out the color in your skin. You're already so handsome, purple shirts will make you irresistible. Women will look at those shirts and imagine themselves running their hands up and down your chest."

"Your first lesson is this, women are as beautiful as men make them feel they are. I want you to learn how to make women feel beautiful."

"What about married women? Shouldn't I keep away from them?" he asked.

"Why? Roger, for every cheating man there is a woman cheating with him. It's part of life. Just remember, no man ever stole another man's woman. She went willingly. And, usually, because she wasn't being treated the right way."

"What about men? Do women ever steal men?"

"All the time. Men are weak and stupid and they think with their penises. That's what makes them so lovable. Remember Roger, sex is never free. It always has a price

216

attached and you want to know the price before you buy. Think before you act. You never know what the consequences of your actions might be. Never do something you might regret later. Just because you can get a woman to go to bed with you doesn't mean you should do it. There are always consequences."

"That makes it sound dirty."

"I never pass judgment on what consenting adults do. Besides, there is a lot more to sex than physical intimacy," she told him. "Watch out for women who don't like it. They'll make your life miserable. There is more to life than sex, but sex is a big part of it and anyone that doesn't enjoy it should be avoided."

"So, everyone cheats?"

"No, there are some people that really are faithful. Still, they like to flirt, especially women. Women love the idea that a man thinks they're beautiful. All women want to be beautiful. Make them feel beautiful and they'll love you for it. But, there's more. I'll teach you how to be kind and loving to them. Do all of that for a woman and she'll do anything for you. Even married women."

"And, if she is one of those women who doesn't cheat? What if I flirt and make her feel beautiful and she doesn't go to bed with me? What then?"

"Trust that woman completely. She'll be a true friend. Now, take my clothes off. Slowly. I'm going to show you how to pleasure a woman's body."

"You're like some kind of man whisperer," he said as he slowly unbuttoned her blouse. "Like one of those Indians who can talk with animals and get them to do things, except you do it with men."

She smiled at that. "Yes, and I'm going to teach you how to be a woman whisperer."

She watched with pleasure as he slowly kissed her body, working his way down her chest. She groaned and arched her back to meet him as he sucked her nipples into his mouth.

"I love your breasts, Raphaela. They're so beautiful."

"Oh, Roger! We're going to have so much fun."

217

Epilogue

The caretaker at the cemetery became accustomed to women asking directions to Roger's grave in the years after his death. So much so he made copies of a map showing the location. Each of the women were different. Some were tall, others were short. Slender and curvy. Young and old. Blonds, brunettes, redheads.

He would respect their privacy by working somewhere else, but he saw enough to know they reacted differently when at his grave. Some would stand. Others would sit by his grave in solitary grief. Occasionally, one would lie down on the grass, as if trying to give him one last hug. Some, he could see, would talk to the man who was no longer there. Others simply wept in silence. Many of them left flowers.

He didn't notice at first, but he soon realized there was one thing they all had in common – instead of being dressed in traditional black, they wore something purple, as if they had made an agreement between themselves.

He called them the Purple Legion.

Made in the USA
Middletown, DE
31 May 2017